"A particular end-times scenario has becom  ture—particularly thanks to the Left Behir Harold Camping, and others—that we forg cultural phenomenon that has replaced biblical truth. Halsted provides a welcome and welcoming invitation to re-examine what so many Christians think they know about the end times based on this cultural edifice in light of a careful examination of the texts in scripture from which it has been constructed, urging us to care about the contextual meaning of each of its diverse building blocks. At the same time, he makes room for a more genuinely biblical eschatology that keeps us looking forward with confidence, not fear, to the consummation of our hope when Christ returns."

DAVID A. DESILVA, Trustees' Distinguished Professor of
New Testament and Greek, Ashland Theological Seminary

"'The Rapture,' the 'Antichrist,' the 'Great Tribulation,' the 'Mark of the Beast,' '666': as our world seems to be unraveling and people are becoming more and more anxious, we are hearing these terms being talked about with increasing frequency. In this well-researched, well-written, and forcefully argued book, Matthew Halsted considers these and other aspects of the standard evangelical 'rapture' eschatology and holds them up to the light of biblical scholarship and reason. In the process, Halsted not only deconstructs the standard evangelical understanding of these concepts, he demonstrates how these and other biblical images of the end times were meant to buttress our hope in Christ's second coming, not to instill us with fear. Anyone who has ever embraced or been influenced by the standard evangelical eschatology, or who knows people who have, needs to read this compelling and much-needed book!"

GREG BOYD, senior pastor of Woodland Hills Church, St. Paul, MN

"Confused by the claims and codewords of a Left Behind generation? Worried that you—or they—might be missing out on key Bible emphases? Matthew Halsted uses plain language to distill and decode popular and scholarly thinking about seven(!) common questions concerning the alleged end times."

ANDREW MALONE, lecturer in biblical studies, Ridley College, Australia

"In the wrong hands, Revelation can be a dangerous book. Seeking to prevent further harm and to do good, Matthew Halsted insightfully and pastorally examines seven common questions about Revelation—an appropriate number for this book full of sevens. Grounded in solid scholarship but written in understandable prose, Halsted's book should be read by anyone with questions about Revelation and other biblical texts concerning the end times. Readers may not agree with everything, but they will know the issues and have lots to chew on."

MICHAEL J. GORMAN, Raymond E. Brown Chair in Biblical Studies and Theology, St. Mary's Seminary and University, Baltimore

"No topic is more controversial than our understanding of how the world will end—especially in Christian theology. Matthew Halsted's carefully guided tour of the relevant biblical passages and how they fit together provides a gentle yet challenging corrective to some of our most popular yet misguided takes on the end times. This book is biblically grounded, carefully reasoned, and above all, an absolute joy to read—even if you're not a seasoned theologian."

MARK BEUVING, pastor of Creekside Church, Rocklin, CA; author of *Multiply: Disciples Making Disciples* (with Francis Chan)

"Anchored in solid scholarship, this accessible guide to Revelation and other biblical prophecy invites us to avoid speculation and focus on living the way of the Lamb in our present. Halsted shows why it is important to consider the original context of apocalyptic and prophetic texts before applying their message to our lives and our times."

J. NELSON KRAYBILL, author of *Apocalypse and Allegiance: Worship, Politics, and Devotion in the Book of Revelation*

THE END
of the
WORLD
as You Know It

WHAT THE BIBLE REALLY SAYS
ABOUT THE END TIMES
(AND WHY IT'S GOOD NEWS)

THE END
of the
WORLD
as You Know It

**WHAT THE BIBLE REALLY SAYS
ABOUT THE END TIMES
(AND WHY IT'S GOOD NEWS)**

MATTHEW L. HALSTED

LEXHAM PRESS

The End of the World as You Know It:
What the Bible Really Says about the End Times (And Why It's Good News)

Copyright 2023 Matthew L. Halsted

Lexham Press, 1313 Commercial St., Bellingham, WA 98225
LexhamPress.com

Print ISBN 9781683597124
Digital ISBN 9781683597131
Library of Congress Control Number 2023938802

Lexham Editorial: Elliot Ritzema, Mandi Newell
Cover Design: Joshua Hunt
Typesetting: Justin Marr

To my amazing children: Isaac, Gracie, Hannah, Simon

CONTENTS

ABBREVIATIONS

AB	The Anchor Bible
Ant.	*Jewish Antiquities. Josephus: The Complete Works.* Translated by William Whiston. Nashville: Thomas Nelson, 1998.
BBR	*Bulletin for Biblical Research*
BCL	Bohn's Classical Library
BECNT	Baker Exegetical Commentary on the New Testament
CBQ	*Catholic Biblical Quarterly*
COQG	Christian Origins and the Question of God
DBT	Discovering Biblical Texts
Dom.	Suetonius, *Domitianus*
ECNT	Exegetical Commentary on the New Testament
JETS	*Journal of the Evangelical Theological Society*
J.W.	*Jewish Wars. Josephus: The Complete Works.* Translated by William Whiston. Nashville: Thomas Nelson, 1998.
LCL	Loeb Classical Library
LXX	Septuagint
NCBC	The New Cambridge Bible Commentary
NIB	New Interpreter's Bible
NIBC	New International Biblical Commentary
NICNT	New International Commentary on the New Testament
NIGTC	New International Greek Testament Commentary
NIVAC	New International Version Application Commentary

NTM	New Testament Monographs
NTS	*New Testament Studies*
NTT	New Testament Theology
ONTC	Osborne New Testament Commentaries
OTP	*The Old Testament Pseudepigrapha*. Edited by James H. Charlesworth. 2 vols. New York: Doubleday, 1983.
Pan.	Pliny, *Panegyricus*
PNTC	Pillar New Testament Commentary
TDNT	*Theological Dictionary of the New Testament*. Edited by Gerhard Kittel and Gerhard Friedrich. Translated by Geoffrey W. Bromiley. 10 vols. Grand Rapids: Eerdmans, 1964–1976.
WBC	Word Biblical Commentary

INTRODUCTION

Mushroom clouds. *Nuclear winter. Mass death. Cosmic destruction. Worldwide famine.* These are some of the images that come to mind when people hear the words "the end times." In popular culture, there is a fascination with *the end.* For many, the agents of demise are climate change, the rise of political extremism, the proliferation of weapons of mass destruction—to name but a few candidates.

But a fascination with the end of the world is found not just in popular culture. In Christianity, the interest may be even more intense. Christians throughout history have had an attraction to the end times, mainly because one core hope of Christianity is the belief that one day God will deal with the problem of sin and evil. And this is something that happens at *the end of time.*

Theology that deals with the end times is known as *eschatology*, a term that comes from two Greek words: *eschatos* ("end") and *logos* ("word" or "study"). Together, they mean "the study of the last things." Eschatology isn't always a source of hope for Christians, though; it has a tendency to stir up a cocktail of fear and angst. After all, disaster and judgment do not exactly invite mushy feelings for many people.

But I suspect this fear and angst also come from the strangeness of the topic. Many passages in the Bible that are classified as eschatological are often filled with puzzling language, mythical characters, and hard-to-grasp symbols. Take Revelation, for instance. This mysterious book documents the visions of a man named John, who witnesses a host of strange things. He tells of gargoyle-like, multiwinged creatures that stand before a throne, perpetually praising God (Rev 4:6–8). He describes a slain lamb with seven horns and seven eyes (Rev 5:6). He speaks even of a pregnant woman who wears the sun

1

like a dress, as well as a seven-headed dragon that stands ready to eat her baby as soon as she gives birth (Rev 12:4).

John's descriptions can seem rather nightmarish. The dragon, for example, aims to destroy Christians by waging a merciless war against them (Rev 12:17). To do so, he empowers two beasts—one that rises out of the sea and one that comes from the earth (Rev 13). The first demands worship from people, while the second promotes this by erecting an image of the first. People are then forced to either worship the image or face the death penalty (13:12–15). Those who devote themselves to the Beast are marked with the Beast's name, which is depicted in the number 666—the infamous "mark of the beast" (13:16–18).

In light of this, it is understandable that many Christians find Revelation—and eschatology in general—to be confusing, frightening, *and* interesting all at the same time.

A FEARFUL MISUNDERSTANDING

I suspect much of the fear around the end times is not due to the strangeness of these passages or even the prospect of judgment as much as it is due to misunderstandings about their purpose and context. When it comes to the end times, many Christians tend to focus on things such as the mysterious figure known as the Antichrist. *Who is he? When will he show up? Is he already in power?* The mark of the Beast also gets a lot of attention. *Is it a microchip? Social Security cards? Vaccines?* These questions give rise to a lot of speculative theories, and these theories leave many Christians living in fear. Especially if they believe they are living as the final generation in the end times, Christians spread these (and other) speculative theories to their friends, which in turn spreads fear even more.

But if people are reading end-times texts and walking away with worry and dread, something is wrong. In fact, I would say that they are most likely *mis*reading these texts. Revelation was *not* meant to produce fear but rather joy, peace, and hope. The same can be said about other end-times texts. The focus is never doom and gloom but faith and confidence. So while the motivations behind people's speculations are almost always sincere, this is not enough. If sincerity is not coupled with knowledge and discernment, it can lead people to act irresponsibly. It can even be dangerous.

Through the years, I have for the most part stayed silent instead of speaking against some of the speculations being made by many Christians and by my fellow evangelicals in particular. I simply didn't want to upset anybody or create division. But I have come to realize that much harm is done to the body of Christ when believers believe and share speculative ideas without evidence to back them up. This is especially true given that many church leaders—pastors, elders, deacons—are themselves guilty of spreading unhelpful views about the end times. When this happens, the gospel's image is affected—even when this spreading of ideas is done sincerely. The church (and above all her leaders) should know better.

Sadly, some speculative preachers have a large audience, allowing them to do a lot of damage when they turn out to be wrong. One well-known American televangelist, for example, claimed that God revealed to him that Donald Trump would win his reelection bid in 2020. He further stated that Trump's second term would be in connection with various end-time prophecies about Israel in particular and the world in general. He even went so far as to speculate how these events would lead to an asteroid smashing into the earth.[1] Yet, none of this ended up happening. Claims such as this illustrate something peculiar about modern prophetic speculation, namely, that it's fairly self-centered. *We* live in a special time; *we* are the last generation; *we* are the ones who will see the end of the world. Perhaps it's not too much to say that modern prophecy appears self-absorbed.

But this sort of speculation is not unique to the twentieth and twenty-first centuries. Christopher Columbus, for example, was motivated to sail across the Atlantic to the New World by his own

---

1. CBN News, "Pat Robertson Prophecy: Here's Who Will Win Election, Then End Times Prophecies Will Unfold," YouTube, 12:26, October 20, 2020, https://youtu.be/LAUbsx5iUFk.

me-centered speculations about the end times. Columbus was convinced that God had called him to help usher in "the imminent new heaven and earth prophesied in Scripture."[2] Some in the Reformation era had similarly self-absorbed views about the end:

> Melchior Hoffman courageously returned to Strassburg, accepting his arrest, because he expected it to become the new Jerusalem; he died there ten years later. An extremist then announced that Münster would become the new Jerusalem, crowned himself David, and reestablished polygamy, leading to the rapid slaughter of everyone in the city by Lutherans. Thomas Müntzer took part in the Peasant's Revolt of 1524, expecting this to be the final judgment; but after six thousand peasants died he was captured and executed. In those days end-time miscalculations often died hard, unfortunately quite literally.[3]

Others such as Hanserd Knollys, a seventeenth-century English Baptist, thought that "the street of the great city" cited in Revelation 11:8 was a reference to London.[4] Benjamin Keach was another Baptist who lived during the ascendancy of William of Orange to the English throne. With William as king, Catholicism took a big hit in England, pushing Rome's authority to the periphery. Keach subsequently thought William's reign was connected to the outpouring of God's wrath mentioned in Revelation 16. He thus believed God had used William in his own time to punish the Antichrist, which he took to be Roman Catholicism.[5]

Today's speculative misapplications continue in the same vein. Sadly, the consequences have been dire—not to mention embarrassing. As Christians, we are called to be ambassadors of the King (2 Cor

---

2. Craig S. Keener, *Revelation*, NIVAC (Grand Rapids: Zondervan, 2000), 61.

3. Keener, *Revelation*, 62.

4. Kenneth G. C. Newport, *Apocalypse and Millennium: Studies in Biblical Eisegesis* (Cambridge: Cambridge University Press, 2000), 33.

5. Newport, *Apocalypse and Millennium*, 35–42, esp. 39.

5:20).[6] But this calling is seriously undermined when we propagate false interpretations in front of an unbelieving world. When we buy into (and spread) the teachings of popular prophecy teachers whose predictions fail to pan out, the watching world takes note of our folly. When we share baseless end-times speculations to our friends on social media, unbelievers may very well wonder whether they should listen to the other things we say. Why should they believe our *good news* when we in the same breath spread *fake news*?

TO THEM, BUT FOR US

Why do we find such end-times speculation so tempting? The heart of the problem is that many modern Christians think the Bible was written *to* them. But such thinking isn't correct. The Bible was not written to modern, twenty-first-century people. It was written to people in the ancient world. Of course, it was written *for* everyone's encouragement and growth in the faith, but that is different. Ephesians, for example, was not written to you and me; it was written to the first-century church at Ephesus. Colossians was not written to us, either; it was written to the first-century church at Colossae. Yet, it is still true that Ephesians and Colossians contain very important truths *for* us today.

This "to them, but for us" distinction may seem like splitting hairs, but it's actually important to consider. If we fail to make it, our reading of the Bible will be skewed—and seriously so. Since the Bible was written *to* ancient people, we modern readers must respect the text's original context. We need to become familiar with the text's original audience—with *their* times, *their* situations, *their* assumptions. Otherwise, we rob the text of its context. Yet this is the very thing we do when we believe the Bible was written *to* us. When we think

---

6. Unless otherwise noted, all English quotations from Scripture are taken from the ESV. For the Greek NT, Greek OT, and Hebrew OT, I use Barbara Aland et al., eds., *Novum Testamentum Graece*, 28th ed. (Stuttgart: Deutsche Bibelgesellschaft, 2012); Alfred Rahlfs and Robert Hanhart, *Septuaginta: Id est Vetus Testamentum graece iuxta LXX interpretes*, Editio altera (Stuttgart: Deutsche Bibelgesellschaft, 2006); and K. Elliger and W. Rudolph, eds., *Biblia Hebraica Stuttgartensia*, 5th ed. (Stuttgart: Deutsche Bibelgesellschaft, 1997), respectively, unless indicated otherwise.

this way, the Bible tends to become all about us—about *our* times, *our* situations, *our* assumptions.[7]

When we prioritize our context and exclude the text's original context, we risk muting the text's message, leaving it without a voice of its own. That would be like having a conversation with someone without ever giving them a chance to reply. You will never learn anything from the other person if the conversation becomes all about you. Yet, this is how a lot of people read their Bibles. *They dominate the conversation.* They impose their own modern views and assumptions onto the text. But again, this won't work because the Bible is not a modern book; it's an ancient book that is filled with ancient words, symbols, and concepts. It's okay to think *creatively* and *imaginatively* about how we can apply the Bible to our modern context. The problem, though, is when we do this without any guidance from the Bible's ancient context. Once we take that into account, we will find less need to enter into endless speculations about the future.

Besides, speculations tend to result in rather embarrassing letdowns anyway (as we saw above). Many Christians have been forced to change their interpretations over time. Like I said earlier, people used to think Social Security numbers were the mark of the Beast. But few people talk about that today. Instead, attention has now turned to newer technology. As time goes on, I suspect even these modern speculations will, like others before them, be cast to the wayside for something else.

We could save ourselves much disappointment if we realized that even a text such as that about the mark of the Beast in Revelation was not written to us. Later on, when we learn about the original context of that passage, we will see how easy it was for its original audience to understand. We will learn, for example, how Revelation assumes a person with "wisdom" and "understanding" can actually "calculate the

---

7. See the similar comments in David A. deSilva, *Unholy Allegiances: Heeding Revelation's Warning* (Peabody, MA: Hendrickson, 2013), 2–4. DeSilva is correct when he says that, with respect to Revelation specifically, "this book is *not* in fact about *us*" (3, emphasis original).

number of the beast" and therefore discover its identity (Rev 13:18). In other words, it's not as cryptic a text as one might think.

In fact, Revelation was not written to hide truth, but to reveal truth—hence the title "Revelation." It was written with the assumption that it could be understood. This doesn't mean the original audience had everything figured out or that they found none of it mysterious. But at the same time, Revelation was far more discernible to ancient people than we might realize, and it did not require them to speculate about the far distant future. In fact, the message of Revelation—as a letter *to them*—was applicable to *their* times. As such, its message was easily understandable. And it could be for us, too, if we didn't over-lay it with our twenty-first-century assumptions—that is, if we didn't make the end times all about us.

This is a hard temptation to resist, because we want the Bible to reassure us. When Christians in the past went through persecution and trials, they often wondered whether their present troubles were in fact part of the events of the end.[8] This makes sense, as people nat-urally tend to interpret Scripture in light of their own circumstances, especially when those circumstances are difficult. We all read biblical texts from our own perspective, from a particular interpretive angle. We all read through a set of lenses, much like people read with glasses.

As interpreters, we all have lenses through which we understand the world around us—whether that be music, plays, movies, or texts such as the Bible. The specific color of the lens is largely determined by our situation, place, and circumstances of life. We all read through lenses because we are historically situated people. We are bound to the traditions that make up our unique interpretive perspective. In other words, none of us are *not* biased.[9] We can't escape it.

But we must be careful not to impose our own bias unilaterally onto the Bible. We need to see interpretation as a two-way street: the

---

8. See, e.g., Keener, *Revelation*, 166–67, 359–60.

9. See my book *Paul and the Meaning of Scripture: A Philosophical-Hermeneutic Approach to Paul's Use of the Old Testament in Romans* (Eugene, OR: Pickwick, 2022) for a detailed analysis of interpretive theory.

context of the biblical text *and* the context of the modern interpreter engage in a conversation of sorts—a back-and-forth dialogue, where each informs the other. The text's assumptions must be allowed to enter into meaningful dialogue with the modern reader's assumptions. When we do not let the Bible have its own voice, we risk imposing our own voice onto it. That's what we do when we speculate about the end times using texts such as Revelation.

SEEING FROM THE JESUS ANGLE

Interpreting the Bible is like putting together puzzle pieces to form a picture. If every puzzle piece is not properly placed, then the image will never appear. Readers supply some of the puzzle pieces by bringing their own assumptions to the text. However, because our assumptions are *modern* assumptions, the pieces may not snap together without some tension.

This tension isn't necessarily a bad thing, but if we discover that the image created by our interpretation is distorted or skewed, then it may be smart to take a step back and reevaluate whether we've unwisely forced a puzzle piece in the wrong place. We may need to revise our assumptions so that we can better recreate the image on the puzzle box.

But what if we don't have the right puzzle pieces to begin with? What if we don't have the right assumptions we need to complete the puzzle—that is, to discover meaning in the text? What if we don't even know what the final image is supposed to look like?

Like I said above, our assumptions come from our life context— that is, from our families, denominational traditions, cultures, and so on. We all know, for example, that our *life experiences* shape us into certain sorts of people. But they also shape us as interpreters. Our experiences develop us and form us and, at times, even *re*-form us into what we are today. In short, without experiences, we don't have assumptions. And if we don't have the *right* experiences, then we won't have the *right* assumptions.

This is why we may not be able to understand everything the Bible has to say about the end times. We might not have the right assumptions required for interpreting prophecy accurately. We don't have these assumptions simply because we lack the experiences that make them possible. Many of the details in Scripture about the second coming of Christ, for example, are too mysterious and vague to understand—until, that is, we actually experience the coming of Christ. Then and only then will we be able to go back and reread those texts in light of Christ's return and properly understand them. Only then will we have the right assumptions (puzzle pieces) to see the full picture.

That's why the best way to read prophetic texts in the Bible is *backward*—that is, in light of the second advent of Christ. This is what I call reading from "the Jesus angle." Some Old Testament texts that prophesied about his first coming were mysterious, too. But when Jesus came, those texts gained clarity. The same will be true about texts that forecast his second coming. Some things we simply can't know until he comes again. In the meantime, though, we can still read from the Jesus angle by paying close attention to how Jesus himself interprets end-times passages. This is part of what it means to dig into the Bible's original context. How did a first-century Jew such as Jesus understand prophecy? We can gain a lot of clarity by asking this simple question. The advantage of doing this is that it keeps our modern assumptions in check. It reminds us that it is *not* all about us. It's about Jesus.

THE GAME PLAN

In all my years growing up hearing about Revelation, I never once heard a discussion about its original context. I was taught that Revelation (and all end-times prophecy) was about *my* near future. The original context didn't matter much—if at all. That's why prophecy teachers were always quick to find Bible verses that matched *current* political happenings, especially those in the Middle East. Though I didn't realize it at the time, most of the passages they cited were often used in a way that would have made no sense to the original audience. But why should prophecy teachers have paid any attention to the Bible's ancient context when, after all, their working assumption was that those passages were all about our era? I came to realize that much of what passed as prophecy teaching was actually just guessing. Sadly, despite the zeal of these teachers, their speculations never amounted to much in the end (no pun intended).

In this book, I want to adopt a much different strategy. I want to guide you through the historical context of the Bible's most important end-times texts. Instead of speculating about the future, I want us to think about the present and the future by first returning to the past. We will journey to the first-century era of the Roman Empire—to the Jerusalem of Jesus's day and to Asia Minor (modern-day Turkey), where texts such as Revelation originated. We will discover what life was like for early Christians living in cities such as Thyatira, Ephesus, Pergamum, Smyrna, and the like. Becoming familiar with the religious and cultural background of this era is vital. If we want to understand the end-times texts of the Bible, we have to become familiar with the ancient contexts of the Bible. There's no way around it.

I have two goals for this book. First, I want to teach you how to apply what the Bible says about the end times to your own context. Perhaps you will find that the Bible's message of hope is exactly what you need for your unique situation. When you learn about the historical context of Revelation, for example, you will see how challenging it was for Christians to live in a first-century city such as Ephesus. Maybe you currently find yourself struggling to follow Jesus in the midst of twenty-first-century temptations and trials. If so, I'm convinced you will find good friends among the believers to whom Revelation was written. They can teach us a lot about faith, hope, and love in the midst of trial.

Second, I want to equip you to better discern good end-times teaching from bad teaching. There's a lot of bad teaching out there! To do this, my goal is to stretch you to think critically and carefully about this topic. That's why you will find notes and references to highly respected biblical scholars and theologians on nearly every page. My goal is not to bog you down with loads of information. I simply want to bridge the gap between scholarly work and the church.

I've grown dismayed at how little the work of scholars has made its way into the church. And I've been profoundly discouraged by how much misguided teaching has made its way in. I want to change that.

To do so, I will dare to question common views about the end times, submitting them to the authority of Scripture. I will put to the test a variety of popular assumptions about the end times, such as the idea there will be a future rapture followed by a seven-year tribulation. I will critique the common belief that the mark of the Beast is going to be a physical mark at the end of time, as well as the assumption that Revelation is all about the future.

Where will this investigation lead us? It's too soon to tell. But one thing I can say is that it's always healthy to take what we think we know about the end times and place it into submission before God's word. That's the goal. It's a risky move, though. We may discover we've been wrong about some things. Or we may see we've been correct all along. Either way, it's always a good idea to test the assumptions that undergird our beliefs.

So, grab your favorite beverage, find a good chair, and get comfortable. We're about to travel through the pages of Scripture together. Perhaps you will discover that *the end of the world as you know it* is quite different from the end of the world as Scripture teaches.

1

ARE WE IN THE END TIMES?

Many christians, such as Tim LaHaye and Jerry Jenkins, authors of the popular Left Behind novels, believe that when the Bible talks about the end times, it means the brief season of time associated with Jesus's return. They believe much of the Bible's end-times language has to do with the final events themselves—with either "the end of the Tribulation" (and "the Glorious Appearing") or "the end of the church age," which will take place when believers are raptured out of the world.[1] Though they admit some exceptions to the rule, LaHaye and Jenkins think the Bible's discussions about the end "usually refer to any point from just prior to the Rapture to the Glorious Appearing itself."[2] They calculate this to be a brief period of time—around seven to ten years or so.[3]

---

1. Tim LaHaye and Jerry B. Jenkins, *Are We Living in the End Times? Current Events Foretold in Scripture … and What They Mean,* updated and expanded ed. (Carol Stream, IL: Tyndale House, 2011), 16–17. They admit there are "at least two exceptions" to this in Scripture. They mention Heb 1:1–2 and 1 John 2:18 (p. 17).

2. LaHaye and Jenkins, *End Times,* 19. See also Mark Hitchcock, who says, "I use the term 'end times' to describe the future period of time beginning with the Rapture of the church. We do not live in the end times, but there are events foreshadowing the end times and setting the stage for their coming. These developments are what we often refer to as 'signs of the times.' Not every minor incident is a sign, but there are major events that point toward what lies ahead." See Hitchcock, *The End: A Complete Overview of Bible Prophecy and the End of Days* (Carol Stream, IL: Tyndale House, 2012), 46. Hitchcock makes a distinction "between the 'last days' for the church, which we are in now, and the last days for Israel, which is still in the future" (95). For him, the church's last days will end at the rapture, which simultaneously launches the last days for Israel. The "end times," he says, "is a broad umbrella term" that describes "all the events beginning with the Rapture all the way to eternity" (96; see also 97–102).

3. See LaHaye and Jenkins, *End Times,* 17–19, 25.

Such thinking is popular among evangelicals—not least because of the soaring success the Left Behind series has enjoyed the past several decades. The books have sold millions of copies. LaHaye and Jenkins's powerful storytelling abilities have captivated the masses and effectively enraptured (pun intended) a loyal base of followers in the process. But is this view, that the end times is limited to the handful of years leading up to the return of Jesus, correct? To find out, let's take a closer look at what the Bible means when it talks about the end times.

FINDING THE RIGHT ENDING

To begin, we need to pay careful attention to the different terms the biblical authors use when they speak about the end times. In the Old Testament, we encounter phrases such as "the end of the days" (Dan 12:13), "the day of the LORD" (Joel 2:1, 31), and "the latter days" (Mic 4:1; Isa 2:2). In the New Testament, we come across phrases such as "the last days" (Acts 2:17), "the last hour" (1 John 2:18), "the end of the age" (Matt 24:3), "the end" (Matt 24:6), and "the day of the Lord" (1 Thess 5:2).

Each of these phrases refers to the end times, but when we take a look at their context we discover not all of them are about the final events before Jesus's return. How can this be? The answer is simple: the end times is not just about the final events. *The end* is not all about the future—at least not in the way most people think. To see what's going on, let's take a deep dive into some of these texts, beginning first with the Old Testament.

THE END TIMES IN THE OLD TESTAMENT

There are many Old Testament texts that predict events that will happen in both the original writer's future *and* our own. Consider this passage from Daniel: "And many of those who sleep in the dust of the earth shall awake, some to everlasting life, and some to shame and everlasting contempt. And those who are wise shall shine like the brightness of the sky above; and those who turn many to righteousness, like the stars forever and ever" (Dan 12:2–3).[4] Here Daniel gets a glimpse into the future, both his and ours. This passage most likely refers to the final, bodily resurrection of both the righteous and the wicked at the end of time.[5]

Later in the chapter, we see the same thing: "But go your way till the end. And you shall rest and shall stand in your allotted place at the end of the days" (Dan 12:13). This verse describes Daniel's eventual death and his resurrection afterward.[6] In the Greek version of this verse, the word "arise" (*anistēmi*) is used instead of "stand" (Dan 12:13 LXX). This is the word for resurrection, and it's the same word Jesus uses to refer to the *final* resurrection at the end of time in John 6:40.[7] So when Daniel talks about "the end of the days," he's likely referring to the resurrection *at the end of time*, which is an event in his future *and* ours.

We see the same thing in Micah 4:1 with the phrase "the latter days." This phrase occurs within the context of a discussion about God's judgment. When God's judgment is accomplished, says Micah, the entire world will be absent of war and full of peace:

> He shall judge between many peoples,
>   and shall decide for strong nations far away;
> and they shall beat their swords into plowshares,
>   and their spears into pruning hooks;
> nation shall not lift up sword against nation,

---

4. On why the text says "many" and not "all" are resurrected, Anthony A. Hoekema says, "It is probably correct to say that the resurrection Daniel predicts is here limited to Israelites; this, however, is not surprising in view of the fact that in the prophets Israel stands for the people of God, and any message about the people of God has to be expressed in terms of Israel. In any event, we have here explicit Old Testament teaching about a resurrection of the body which will be both to everlasting life and to eternal condemnation." Hoekema, *The Bible and the Future* (Grand Rapids: Eerdmans, 1994), 245. Compare Isa 26:19.

5. See, e.g., Hoekema, *Bible and the Future*, 240, 245.

6. John J. Collins, *Daniel: A Commentary on the Book of Daniel* (Minneapolis: Augsburg Fortress, 1993), 401 (see also 402).

7. "For this is the will of my Father, that everyone who looks on the Son and believes in him should have eternal life, and I will raise [*anistēmi*] him up on the last day [*eschatē hēmera*]" (John 6:40).

neither shall they learn war anymore;
but they shall sit every man under his vine and under his fig tree,
and no one shall make them afraid,
for the mouth of the LORD of hosts has spoken.
(Mic 4:3–4)[8]

Isaiah says the same thing. He, too, speaks about "the latter days" (Isa 2:2) as a vision for the same world peace Micah spoke about above: "He shall judge between the nations, and shall decide disputes for many peoples; and they shall beat their swords into plowshares, and their spears into pruning hooks; nation shall not lift up sword against nation, neither shall they learn war anymore" (Isa 2:4).[9]

A brief glance at the news suggests that none of these prophecies has come true yet. The world is far from the sort of peace Micah and Isaiah envisioned. When they spoke about the end times, they were referring to the time of the final events. They are talking about events in their future *and* our own. This shows clearly how the Bible teaches that "the end times" refers to the future—about events that have *yet* to happen.

But there's more to the story. The Bible *also* speaks about the end times as something that has already arrived.

JOEL'S VISION OF THE END TIMES

When the Old Testament prophet Joel talks about the end times, he uses the phrase "the day of the LORD" (1:15; 2:1). In its original context, this phrase had to do with an invasion of locusts that had swarmed the land, decimating everything in its path—farms, vineyards, orchards,

---

8.   Ralph Smith says Mic 4:1–5 "is freighted with eschatological overtones" and "concerns the remote future" with respect to the original oracle. See Smith, *Micah–Malachi*, WBC (Waco, TX: Word, 1984), 36–37. He adds that this passage "looks forward to the day when the enmity that separated the nations at Babel (Gen 11) will be put aside and all peoples of the world will worship the one true God. They will be taught Yahweh's law and not the ways of war. A universal reign of peace will prevail and each individual will participate in it (v 4)" (37).

9.   On the relationship between Isa 2:2–4 and Mic 4:1–5, see the discussion in Smith, *Micah–Malachi*, 37.

and the like (Joel 1:2–12).[10] The devastation caused by the plague was an act of divine judgment, for Joel uses the occasion to call for fasting, crying, and repentance (1:13–20).[11]

In the next chapter, Joel offers more details. He starts by saying "the day of the LORD is coming" (2:1). He describes it as "a day of darkness and gloom, a day of clouds and thick darkness! Like blackness there is spread upon the mountains a great and powerful people" (2:2a). This "powerful people," he says, resembles "war horses" that are "drawn up for battle" (2:4–5). But Joel is not talking about a literal army. This is clear from 2:25, where God calls the locust plague "my great army." This may explain why Joel describes the "day of the LORD" as "a day of darkness" and as "a day of clouds." Locust swarms can be massive, blanketing large swaths of land in one moment and extending deep shadows on the land beneath. In the late nineteenth century, one locust swarm in the Middle East "was estimated to cover two thousand square miles."[12] No wonder Joel uses the language of catastrophe and destruction when speaking about them.

But I don't think Joel is predicting that the day of the Lord will be another locust plague like the one described in Joel 1. He seems instead to be using the locust invasion as a vivid illustration for the coming day of the Lord.[13] Joel is saying that, like a locust invasion, the day of the Lord will be dramatic and earth-shaking (2:10). This coming "day of the LORD" will be a day of judgment (Joel 1:15; 2:1, 11).

But it's not merely a day of judgment in the negative sense. The first section of Joel 2 depicts the day as a day of wrath (2:2–11), but the second section holds out hope for God's mercy for those who repent (2:12–17).[14] And God's mercy knows no bounds. Joel goes on to say

---

10. Robert B. Chisholm, *Interpreting the Minor Prophets* (Grand Rapids: Zondervan, 1990), 54–55.

11. Locust swarms are a fearsome phenomenon—in both the ancient and modern world. See, e.g., Raymond Dillard, "Joel," in *The Minor Prophets: An Exegetical and Expository Commentary*, ed. Thomas Edward McComiskey (Grand Rapids: Baker, 1992), 255–56.

12. Dillard, "Joel," 256.

13. Dillard, "Joel," 277–78.

14. Chisholm, *Interpreting the Minor Prophets*, 59–60. See also Dillard, "Joel," 266.

that God will "restore to [his people] the years that the swarming locust has eaten" (2:25). Chapter 2 ends with a promise that God will not only restore his people's land, but he will also renew his people once and for all. In doing so, he will visit his people in a special way. Joel 2:28–29 says God will "pour out" his Spirit on his people, leading them to prophesy as well as to have dreams and visions.

You might be wondering what any of this has to do with our topic. As it turns out, it has a lot to do with it. Joel's prophecy played a key role in how the writers of the New Testament understood the end times.[15] To see how, let's jump to the book of Acts.

THE BEGINNING OF THE END TIMES

In Acts 2, the Holy Spirit fell on a group of Christians who were gathered on the Jewish festival of Pentecost, which took place seven weeks after Passover. It was a rather diverse bunch. They hailed from various regions of the world—from Rome, Egypt, Judea, and modern-day Turkey, to name a few places (Acts 2:9–11). Most of these people would have grown up speaking their local dialect as well as Greek (many people were at least bilingual at this time). Knowing Greek had an advantage because a lot of people living across the empire could speak it, so learning Greek would aid in communication across ethnic lines.

But at Pentecost, a miracle occurred. When the Holy Spirit came on the believers, they were enabled to understand each other in their own dialect (Acts 2:6). As a result, everyone was left amazed, shocked, and surprised. Witnessing this event firsthand, the apostle Peter knew exactly what it meant and offered everyone an explanation by quoting from Joel 2:28–32 (Acts 2:16–21).[16] But Peter does not quote Joel's

---

15. So C. M. Blumhofer: "The prophecy of Joel exercised a powerful effect on the early Christian imagination." Blumhofer, "Luke's Alteration of Joel 3.1–5 in Acts 2.17–21," *NTS* 62 (October 2016): 501 (see also 502).

16. On how Luke narrates Peter's speech such that it grants the latter a "prophetic stance," thus creating a remarkable parallel between Joel 1:2 and Acts 2:14, see Blumhofer, "Luke's Alteration of Joel," 502.

prophecy word-for-word. Instead, he makes a few subtle changes. One change occurs in Acts 2:17, where Peter quotes Joel 2:28. Let's compare Peter's quotation with Joel's original text:

> And it shall come to pass *afterward*, that I will pour out my Spirit on all flesh. (Joel 2:28)

> And *in the last days* it shall be, God declares, that I will pour out my Spirit on all flesh. (Acts 2:17)

Peter replaces the word "afterward" with the phrase "in the last days."[17] Apparently, Peter thought his own day was part of the "last days."[18] Even though Scripture can speak about the end times as a reference to the final events of history (as we have seen above), Peter's speech shows how early Christians believed and taught that *they* were living in the time of the end. They believed Joel's prophecy was being fulfilled with the coming of the Holy Spirit.[19] This means that, from our twenty-first-century perspective, the end times is not just something that will come a few years before the final events. To the contrary, *it has already arrived.*

But Joel's prophecy was not fulfilled on just that one day of Pentecost. It was fulfilled continuously in the life of the church in the days, years, and centuries to come.[20] How do we know this?

---

17. For a helpful take on this change (and others) to Joel's prophecy, see again Blumhofer, "Luke's Alteration of Joel," esp. 503–6. Blumhofer says, "On both text-critical and reaction-critical grounds, the additions to Joel are almost certainly the result of Luke's editorial hand" (500). When I attribute the alteration to Peter, I am assuming that Luke—the writer of Acts—has faithfully reproduced Peter's speech.

18. See the discussion in Darrell L. Bock, *Acts*, BECNT (Grand Rapids: Baker Academic, 2007), 112.

19. As Bock says: "The apostles read such texts [as Joel 2] as last-day, kingdom texts and saw themselves in the last days (1 Pet. 1:20; 1 Cor. 10:11; 1 Tim. 4:1; 2 Tim. 3:1; Heb. 1:1–2; 9:26; 1 John 2:18). Since the day of the Lord is also alluded to in this citation, what Peter is really saying here is that the coming of the Spirit is the beginning of 'those days'" (*Acts*, 112). See also Blumhofer, who says, "Luke's changes to Joel 3.1–5 are held together by a single hermeneutical commitment: the belief that God's eschatological restoration of Israel has begun in the community gathered by Jesus Christ and that the effects of that restoration extend to the nations" ("Luke's Alteration of Joel," 501).

20. See Blumhofer, "Luke's Alteration of Joel," 505, where he mentions how "the outpouring of the Spirit represents the continuing ministry of Jesus through his disciples"; see also 510.

First, notice that the prophecy mentions how the Spirit will fall on people and, as a result, they will "prophesy," "dream dreams," and "see visions" (Joel 2:28). While it is true that these sorts of Spirit-enabled miracles were seen on the day of Pentecost, the Spirit did not cease to be poured out once that day was over. In fact, the New Testament teaches that the Spirit *continues* to give believers these and other supernatural gifts. Later in Acts, for example, we read about "prophets and teachers" ministering in the church of Antioch (Acts 13:1). Years after Pentecost, Paul talks about the ongoing ministry of the Spirit. He speaks of the gifts of prophecy, service, teaching, and others (Rom 13:6–8; see also 1 Cor 12:1–11). What this means is that Joel's prophecy is fulfilled in the lives of Christians beyond Pentecost. And if that's true, then the "last days" of which Peter speaks extend beyond that day, too. This means the end times does not start just before Jesus returns. To the contrary, the end times began two thousand years ago.

Notice also that in Peter's quotations from Joel, he mentions more than just the Spirit's enabling of prophecy, seeing visions, and the like. He also mentions how "it shall come to pass that everyone who calls upon the name of the Lord shall be saved" (Acts 2:21, quoting Joel 2:32). I raise this point to show that the Spirit's outpouring predicted by Joel includes more than just supernatural gifts. It also includes salvation becoming available to everyone.[21] Obviously, the gospel was available to more people than just those who were present on the day of Pentecost two thousand years ago. It was available afterward, too. Many years after Pentecost, Paul quotes this same part of Joel's prophecy ("For 'everyone who calls on the name of the Lord will be saved,'" Rom 10:13). Paul assumes Joel's prophecy is continuing to be fulfilled in his time. It's fulfilled in ours, too. Joel's prophecy continues to be fulfilled every time a person comes to faith in Jesus. Why? *Because we are living in the end times.*

---

21. See again Blumhofer, "Luke's Alteration of Joel," 505 (see also 514).

All of this leads naturally into one final observation. In the original context of his prophecy, Joel says God will be "in the midst of Israel" (Joel 2:27). A few verses down, Joel prophesies that God will one day "show wonders in the heavens and on the earth" (2:30). Going back to Peter's speech, it is interesting how he quotes this part of the prophecy. He says, "And I will show wonders in the heavens above and signs on the earth below" (Acts 2:19a).[22] Immediately after his quotation from Joel, Peter begins talking about Jesus to show that the works he did while on earth are the same *wonders* and *signs* that Joel prophesied about. Peter says,

> Men of Israel, hear these words: Jesus of Nazareth, a man attested to you by God with mighty works and wonders and signs that God did through him in your midst, as you yourselves know—this Jesus, delivered up according to the definite plan and foreknowledge of God, you crucified and killed by the hands of lawless men. God raised him up, loosing the pangs of death, because it was not possible for him to be held by it. (Acts 2:22–24)

Peter believes the signs and wonders Jesus did during his life are fulfillments of Joel's oracle.[23] He also points out that it was God who worked these "mighty works and wonders and signs ... through him [Jesus] *in your midst*" (Acts 2:22). This recalls Joel's prophecy that God would one day live "in the midst" (Joel 2:27) of his people,

---

22. Bock thinks "signs" is another addition—along with "above" and "below"—to the prophetic text in order "to complete the parallelism" (*Acts*, 115; compare Blumhofer, "Luke's Alteration of Joel," 510–11). I tend to see the other signs and wonders mentioned in 2:19–20a as references to the ministry of Jesus—specifically, to Jesus's crucifixion ("blood"; compare Rom 5:9), the judgment that has come in Christ's first advent ("fire" and "vapor of smoke"; compare John 12:31–32), and the way in which creation groaned when Jesus was crucified ("sun ... turned to darkness and the moon to blood"; compare Luke 23:44–45). That said, I do not discount the idea that these are intended to foreshadow and anticipate, in some sense, the second coming of Christ. On all of this, I am indebted to the discussion found in Bock, *Acts*, 115–17, although he seems a bit more futuristic than I am comfortable with (see, e.g., 116–17).

23. They are also fulfilled in "the community that invokes his name (4:30)" (Blumhofer, "Luke's Alteration of Joel," 510).

performing "wonders in the heavens" (Joel 2:30; 3:3 LXX). Peter is convinced that Jesus fulfills the prophet's words.[24] This means that the fulfillment of Joel's prophecy is not really about the "when" (at the day of Pentecost) but rather about the "who" (Jesus of Nazareth). In other words, the fulfillment is not so much an event but a person. If the end times is centered on the person and ministry of Jesus, then to be *in Jesus* is to be a *participant in the end times*.

Many years later, Peter continued in this belief that prophecies about the end times had been in one sense fulfilled in Jesus. He writes,

> This is now the second letter that I am writing to you, beloved. In both of them I am stirring up your sincere mind by way of reminder, that you should remember the predictions of the holy prophets and the commandment of the Lord and Savior through your apostles, knowing this first of all, that scoffers will come *in the last days* with scoffing, following their own sinful desires. (2 Pet 3:1–3)

Peter is warning his readers about scoffers who raise doubts about "the promise of his coming" (3:4). Peter goes on to encourage Christians to remember that "the Lord is not slow to fulfill his promise as some count slowness" (3:9). In other words, the Lord *will* return. In the meantime, says Peter, believers are to live holy and upright lives. As they do this, they are "waiting and hastening the coming of the day of God" (3:12). Peter adds that both he and his readers are—in their own time—"waiting" for the new creation (3:13). Peter clearly thought he was living "in the last days" (3:3). Why would Peter need to warn people about scoffers appearing "in the last days" if he thought he was speaking about a time his own readers would never have to worry about?

All of this leads to the conclusion that "end times" means something more than simply *that unique period of time just before the final events*. The end times, apparently, is a season that lasts for hundreds—indeed, thousands—of years.

---

24. Compare the helpful discussion in Bock, *Acts*, 119–20.

WHAT DID OTHER EARLY CHRISTIANS BELIEVE ABOUT THE END TIMES?

Peter was not alone in thinking he was living in the end times. The apostle Paul writes to his protégé Timothy,

> But understand this, that *in the last* [*eschatos*] *days* there will come times of difficulty. For people will be lovers of self, lovers of money, proud, arrogant, abusive, disobedient to their parents, ungrateful, unholy, heartless, unappeasable, slanderous, without self-control, brutal, not loving good, treacherous, reckless, swollen with conceit, lovers of pleasure rather than lovers of God, having the appearance of godliness, but denying its power. Avoid such people. (2 Tim 3:1–5)

Here Paul reminds Timothy not to be surprised when evil people act evil. This is exactly what is supposed to happen "in the last days." A lot like Peter, Paul assumed *he was living in the end times.* The phrase "in the last days" is not a reference to the far distant future. If it were, he would not have told Timothy to "avoid" people of that era (3:5). What would have been the purpose of telling Timothy to avoid people who would live thousands of years after he was dead?

Paul says something similar in his first letter to Timothy:

> Now the Spirit expressly says that in *later* [*hysteros*] *times* some will depart from the faith by devoting themselves to deceitful spirits and teachings of demons, through insincerity of liars whose consciences are seared, who forbid marriage and require abstinence from foods that God created to be received with thanksgiving by those who believe and know the truth. (1 Tim 4:1–3)

Paul does not use the typical Greek word *eschatos* ("last") as he does in 2 Timothy, but *hysteros* ("later") carries the same meaning here. Once again, Paul is not talking about the distant future. He is writing about Timothy's present situation. As the following verses indicate, some were teaching that Christians should not eat some types of food and follow certain dietary practices. In response, Paul says that a person is allowed to eat whatever they wish so long as it is "received with thanksgiving" because "everything created by God is good" and can be "made holy by the word of God and prayer" (1 Tim 4:4–5). When Paul tells Timothy to "put these things" (4:6) before the rest of the church, he's referring to the truths of 1 Timothy 4:4–5. Paul needed to tell Timothy this because of those who believed they should practice "abstinence from foods" of a certain kind (4:2–3). Timothy should not be surprised that people were teaching this because "the Spirit expressly says that in later times" some people would do so (4:1). In other words, Paul thought the "later times" included his own time.

James, Jesus's brother, thinks the same way. In chapter 5 of his letter, James launches a tirade against the rich and the powerful. He accuses some of his readers of hiring workers without paying them appropriately, defrauding them and exploiting their labor (5:1–6). He says they have abused their employees while they themselves live a life of luxury, selfishly storing up "treasure in the last [*eschatos*] days" (5:3). James connects the entire discussion to the second coming of Christ (5:7). This suggests once more that "the last days" is a very long stretch of time—beginning in the first century. James, like Paul and Peter, clearly believed he was living in the end times.

Other writers of the New Testament think so as well. Consider John: "Children, *it is the last* [*eschatos*] *hour*, and as you have heard that antichrist is coming, so now many antichrists have come. Therefore we know that *it is the last* [*eschatos*] *hour*" (1 John 2:18). And Jude:

> But you must remember, beloved, the predictions of the apostles of our Lord Jesus Christ. They said to you, "*In the last* [*eschatos*] *time* there will be scoffers, following their own ungodly passions." It is these who cause divisions, worldly people, devoid of the Spirit. But you, beloved, building yourselves up in your most holy faith and praying in the Holy Spirit, keep yourselves in the love of God, waiting for the mercy of our Lord Jesus Christ that leads to eternal life. (Jude 17–21)

And the author of Hebrews: "Long ago, at many times and in many ways, God spoke to our fathers by the prophets, but *in these last [eschatos] days he has spoken to us by his Son,* whom he appointed the heir of all things, through whom also he created the world" (Heb 1:1–2).

The passage from Hebrews is especially insightful. According to the author of Hebrews, the end times were in full swing at the time of writing: "in *these* last days" (1:2). Notice also how the author connects "these last days" with the life and ministry of Jesus. The first coming of Jesus has brought about a decisive change in human history. This same idea is seen elsewhere in Hebrews. Christ "appeared once for all at the end of the ages to put away sin by the sacrifice of himself" (Heb 9:26). In other words, the ministry of Jesus is the beginning of the end.[25]

But Jesus is not merely a player in the end times. He is so much more: Jesus is the End. In Revelation, Jesus describes himself as the "Alpha and the Omega, the first and the last, the beginning and the end" (Rev 22:13). The entirety of human history is summed up in Christ. He has altered the whole structure of time. As a result, early Christians saw themselves as the people "on whom the end of the ages has come" (1 Cor 10:11). They understood their own time as the end times because Jesus is the one in whom all things have found their end.

So, are we living in the end times? Yes. In fact, we've been living in the end times for the past two thousand years—ever since Jesus first arrived.

THE END IS HERE,
AND THE END IS COMING

Of course, while the end times began two thousand years ago, Jesus has not returned yet. Like I said earlier in the chapter, even though it's true that some end-times passages have already been fulfilled, some have not. Jesus, for example, talks about final events in Matthew 24.[26] Paul does in 1 Corinthians as well. He says,

---

25. See Hoekema, *Bible and the Future,* 17, who says, "In comparison with the provisional role of the Old Testament priests, the Epistle to the Hebrews sees the appearance of Christ in terms of eschatological fulfillment and finality."

26. I address Matt 24 at length in chs. 5–6.

> For as in Adam all die, so also in Christ shall all be made alive.
> But each in his own order: Christ the firstfruits, then at his
> coming those who belong to Christ. *Then comes the end*, when
> he delivers the kingdom to God the Father after destroying
> every rule and every authority and power. For he must reign
> until he has put all his enemies under his feet. The last enemy
> to be destroyed is death. (1 Cor 15:22–26)

Here Paul speaks about the final resurrection, which takes place at the
second coming of Christ. After the great resurrection, Paul says, the
end will come. At that point, God will bring his redemptive plans to
finality. Obviously, this has not happened yet. So, when Paul uses the
word "end" (*telos*), he means something along the lines of "culmination"
or "completion of a goal." He clearly has the future—*his and ours*—in
mind. When it comes to the end times, the Bible teaches that it has
already come *and* that it is still coming. Both aspects are important.

We can begin to make sense of this by looking at 1 Thessalonians 5,
where Paul discusses a familiar phrase that we have already seen: "the
day of the Lord." He says this day will "come like a thief in the night"
(5:2). He warns, however, that some people will not be ready for that
day, and it will come as a surprise to them (5:3). He contrasts these
people with the Thessalonian Christians, whom he calls "children of
light" and "children of the day" (5:5). In contrast to unbelievers, who
"sleep," Christians are to be fully "awake" so they will be ready for the
Lord's return (5:6). This is Christians' appropriate posture, says Paul,
because they already "belong to the day" (5:8).

When Paul says Christians "belong to the day," he is continuing with
his metaphor of being awake and alert, just as a person is ready for the
coming "thief in the night" (5:2). But there is another aspect we need to
consider, too. When Paul says Christians "belong to the *day*," he is also
talking about the coming "*day* of the Lord" (5:2, 8). Even though this
day is *future*, believers in Paul's *present* day are intimately connected
with that future day because they belong to Christ and are beneficiaries
of his gracious blessings. New Testament scholar F. F. Bruce puts it well:

The day had not yet arrived, but believers in Christ were children of day already, by a form of "realized eschatology." The day, in fact, had cast its radiance ahead with the life and ministry of the historical Jesus and the accomplishment of his saving work; when it arrived in its full splendor, they would enter into their inheritance of glory and be manifested as children of day.[27]

Here's another way to put it. In one sense, the end has not *yet* come for believers. In another sense, though, it has *already* come on them because they already participate in the life of Jesus—the one who has already come and the one who is coming still (this is the "realized eschatology" Bruce refers to). Remember, the end times is not so much about an event but a person—Jesus Christ. To be in Christ is to be a participant in the end.

Think of the end times as a large, flowing river. The river's source is the life and work of Jesus, which began at Jesus's first coming. The end times began there. The river flows in an uninterrupted fashion to a large sea, where everything is eventually emptied out, where everything finds its destination. Even though it is all one river, there are various points along the river's flow that are individually unique. While the end times is one long river, various points can be pinpointed along the way— some of which have already been fulfilled; others are yet to be fulfilled.

The Christian family, both past and present, has always existed in that river's flow. Some events are unique to the first Christians (near the source of the river), some events will be unique to later Christians (where the river culminates at the sea), and some events are common to all Christians in all times in all places. To be in the end is to be in the river itself; it is being united to Jesus. In this way, we can say *both* that the end is already here *and* the end is still coming. Scholars often describe this as the "tension between the 'already' and the 'not yet.'"[28]

---

27. F. F. Bruce, *1 & 2 Thessalonians*, WBC (Waco, TX: Word, 1982), 111.

28. Hoekema, *Bible and the Future*, 14. Many theologians like Hoekema recognize how the NT divides the end times into two categories: the "present age" and the "age to come" (18). The *present age* encompasses that time between the first and second comings of Christ, and the *age to come* describes the reality after Christ returns (20). See especially 19, where he discusses

SUMMING THINGS UP

We've seen enough examples to show that the end times is not just about the future. The Bible depicts the end times as a long season that includes our present era and our past. Many prophecy teachers, being so preoccupied with the future, seem to miss this fact. Yet it's one that we can't afford to miss if we don't want our interpretations to get off on the wrong foot. After all, if we start off with false assumptions about the end times, we shouldn't be surprised when we end up with misguided interpretations of end-times texts.

We see this a lot with a book such as Revelation. For many people, the logic works like this: since Revelation is about the end times, and since the end times is all about the future, it follows that the message of Revelation is all about the future. But such reasoning doesn't fit with the way the Bible talks about the end times. Even though I do think Revelation has everything to do with the end times, it's not true that *the end times is all about the future* (as we've seen). But when Revelation is read with this assumption in mind, the logical next step is to treat it as a timeline for future events and hence as a playground for speculation. And if we read Revelation in a way that is contrary to how it was intended to be read, then we miss out on its true message.

When it comes to Revelation, then, it's probably worth asking what we've missed. As it turns out, a lot.

---

how the ages can be differentiated in the NT by their singular and plural use (e.g., "the last days" vs. "the last day"; "the end of the ages" vs. "the end of the age").

2

HOW SHOULD WE UNDERSTAND REVELATION?

Many people are terrified to open the book of Revelation. The dragon, the Beast, his mark, the judgments, the lake of fire— it's a lot to take in. Thomas Jefferson once quipped that Revelation consisted of "the ravings of a Maniac, no more worthy, nor capable of explanation than the incoherences of our own nightly dreams."[1] Similarly, in the preface of his translation of Revelation in 1522, Martin Luther describes the book as "neither apostolic nor prophetic," saying further that he can "in no way detect that the Holy Spirit produced it."[2] After accusing the author of Revelation of being somewhat smug and puzzling, Luther confesses, "My spirit cannot accommodate itself to this book. For me this is reason enough not to think highly of it: Christ is neither taught nor known in it."[3]

---

1. Thomas Jefferson, "From Thomas Jefferson to Alexander Smyth, 17 January 1825," Founders Online, National Archives, https://founders.archives.gov/documents/Jefferson/98-01-02-4882.

2. Martin Luther, *Word and Sacrament 1*, ed. E. Theodore Bachman, Luther's Works 35 (Philadelphia: Muhlenberg, 1960), 398.

3. Luther, *Word and Sacrament 1*, 398–99. Luther later discarded this preface and replaced it with a new one in 1530 that doesn't carry the same negative tone as the first. In fact, he thinks readers can indeed "profit" from the book, particularly in terms of finding "comfort" in the hope it emits, as well as the "warning" it gives with respect to trials and persecution (409). He ends his new preface with: "If only the word of the gospel remains pure among us, and we love and cherish it, we shall not doubt that Christ is with us, even when things are at their worst. As we see here in this book [of Revelation], that through and beyond all plagues, beasts, and evil angels Christ is nonetheless with his saints, and wins the final victory" (411).

These comments are bold, to be sure. But they state out loud what many modern people quietly wonder: *What is going on in this book?*

In light of the confusion and terror the book evokes, it's no wonder that many zealous interpreters are eager to spin Revelation's message in a way that would make Freddy Krueger run to a corner of the room and assume the fetal position. I agree with N. T. Wright and Michael Bird, both respected New Testament scholars, who remark, "Revelation is a strange book, nearly as strange as some of its readers."[4] Sadly, this is true. It is lamentable that Revelation often gets weaponized for the advancement of unsubstantiated conspiracy theories, modern myths, and sundry political views.

In some corners of evangelicalism, there is a particular knack for such speculative approaches to Revelation—and for making them popular, too. In his book *Revelation: A Biography,* Timothy Beal mentions in this regard the hit movie *A Thief in the Night.* This 1970s end-times flick "had a tremendous influence on innumerable American teens." One of its legacies is that it paved the way for what Beal calls "evangelical horror as a genre of film aimed at scaring people into conversion."[5] For many people, the net effect of watching this fictionalized telling of the end times—with symbols and themes from Revelation sprinkled throughout the movie—left people with an enormous amount of *fear.*[6]

Some Christians have a deep angst about the end times as well as a strong reluctance to read texts like Revelation. But this is ironic, since Revelation's original intent was to bring peace and comfort to God's people, not fear. In the words of New Testament scholar Michael Gorman, how we interpret Revelation makes a huge difference in how we see and experience the world:

---

4. N. T. Wright and Michael F. Bird, *The New Testament in Its World: An Introduction to the History, Literature, and Theology of the First Christians* (Grand Rapids: Zondervan, 2019), 808.

5. See Timothy Beal, *Revelation: A Biography,* Lives of Great Religious Books (Princeton: Princeton University Press, 2018), 183, 184.

6. See Beal, *Revelation,* 189–91, where he discusses how there is "cryptic placement of Revelation-related mythemes within the movie's broader pretribulation rapture narrative" (189). He mentions, e.g., the number 666 (189–90), the "armored locusts" (190), and Christ's return at the rapture (190–91). Interestingly, as Beal points out, the rapture is never mentioned in Revelation, though it is often assumed "that the biblical book of Revelation is the blueprint for rapture theory" (177).

How one reads, teaches, and preaches Revelation can have a powerful impact on one's own—and other people's—emotional, spiritual, and even physical and economic well-being. Therefore, interpreting the book of Revelation is a serious and sacred responsibility, not to be entered into lightly. Furthermore, although Scripture is a living word from God that can bring a fresh message to people in changing contexts, with respect to Revelation it must be clearly stated that some readings are not only inferior to others, they are in fact unchristian and unhealthy.[7]

And so we must ask: Is there a better interpretation of Revelation than the one that leaves us in fear and angst? Is there a way to understand it that gives us hope for both the present and future?

READING REVELATION:
THE MISTAKES WE MAKE

As I mentioned in the last chapter, many people assume Revelation is all about the future because it is about the end times. But we've already seen that end-times language in the Bible does not always refer to *our* future. And yet, because people read Revelation with this false assumption in mind, their interpretations result in a plethora of mistakes. While Revelation does have things to say about the future, it was never intended to be read as a play-by-play outline of what is going to happen.

But this is just part of the problem. Another reason people think an end-times book like Revelation is all about the future stems from having a mistaken view about the nature of *prophecy*. Prophecy tends to be associated with "prediction, communicating murky oracles looking off into the distant future, as in the prophecies of Nostradamus that supposedly spoke of events centuries after the time of the speaker."[8] When this assumption is coupled with the fact that Revelation explicitly describes itself as "prophecy" (Rev 1:3), the conclusion is evident:

---

7. Michael J. Gorman, *Reading Revelation Responsibly: Uncivil Worship and Witness: Following the Lamb into the New Creation* (Eugene, OR: Cascade, 2011), xiii–xiv, emphasis original.

8. DeSilva, *Unholy Allegiances*, 5.

Revelation is all about predicting the future. But here's the problem: *biblical prophecy is not primarily about prediction*. David deSilva, a scholar who writes regularly on this issue, says this:

> While such prophecy could include a predictive element, it was also—and perhaps primarily—a declaration of God's actions in the present or an announcement of God's evaluation of the present actions of God's people, diagnosing problems and calling for realignment with God's values. Prophecy is essentially a "word of the Lord" breaking into the situation of the Lord's people who need guidance or encouragement or a call to repentance and recommitment.[9]

While Revelation does concern itself with prediction on some level, there is more to its message than just this. What is its message? Simply put, Revelation invites readers to view the cosmos from God's perspective. It places a call on all people to adopt a new worldview—one that, at its center, has the slain Lamb receiving the glory he deserves. Revelation calls us to do more than speculate about the future. Instead, it calls us to reimagine the *present* with a God's-eye point of view. Revelation offers a grand vision of human history—*past, present,* and *future*—and we should reinterpret it in light of the kingdom of God.

FINDING CLARITY

Sadly, many misguided—albeit sincere—interpreters of Revelation have done a grave disservice to the church. They have wanted to make Revelation relevant to our times, but instead have turned it into a fearful mystery and morphed it into an enigma of anxiety about the future. How can we move beyond the weird, though still very popular, interpretations of Revelation? What is a better interpretive approach? The answer is simple: *we have to read Revelation on its own terms.*

---

9. DeSilva, *Unholy Allegiances*, 6. See also Gorman: "But prophecy, in the biblical tradition, is not exclusively or even primarily about making pronouncements and predictions concerning the future. Rather, prophecy is speaking words of comfort and/or challenge, on behalf of God, to the people of God in their concrete historical situation" (*Reading Revelation*, 23).

If we want Revelation to speak to our modern times with clarity, the first thing we need to do is get to know its original context—specifically, its historical and social setting. We need to familiarize ourselves with the world of Revelation's original audience. We need to acquaint ourselves with their situations and circumstances. By doing so, we modern, twenty-first-century readers will be confronted with how we have perhaps incorrectly imposed our own modern assumptions on Revelation's text, thus obscuring its true meaning. Ironically, people who think Revelation is all about the future have so distorted the original message of Revelation that they have muted its ability to speak meaningfully in today's (and tomorrow's) world.

That's why we need to work hard to enter into the world of the Christians living in Asia Minor. We want to become familiar with *their* world, *their* context, and *their* story. By doing so, we will find a launching point for us to take Revelation's message to our world. Then and only then can we begin to weave its truth creatively into our modern context. How could we ever hope to apply Revelation's mark of the Beast to our times if we ignore how it was understood in the ancient world?

In the rest of this chapter, I will offer a simple, two-step approach for reading Revelation. This will equip you to cut through all the fearful misrepresentation. By first looking at how it would have been understood by its original readers, you will discover that Revelation has just as much (if not more) to say about the *present* era as it does about the distant future. Far from being scary, you'll see how it's full of comfort and relevant application for today—and all time.

STEP 1: CONSIDER THE
LITERARY CONTEXT

The first thing to do when you sit down to read Revelation is to think about its *literary context*. By this, I mean the *type* of writing Revelation is. Another word for this is *genre*. The reason we need to pay attention to the genre of Revelation is because if we don't, we may misunderstand its message—either completely or partially.

For example, if a person were to read C. S. Lewis's The Chronicles of Narnia without knowing it was fiction, they would miss important elements they otherwise would have caught. If they thought Narnia was historical nonfiction, they would neither understand nor enjoy the message (or the morals) the author intended to communicate. In such cases, the regular elements of fantasy (e.g., magic, mythic creatures, etc.) would not—indeed, *could not*—be appreciated by the reader because they would be too busy thinking the author was delusional.

Here's a good rule of thumb: if you want to understand the *message* of Revelation, you need to understand the *genre* of Revelation. Becoming familiar with its genre is not optional. It's essential. So, what is the genre of Revelation? Revelation falls into three distinct yet complementary literary categories. It is a *letter*, an *apocalypse*, and a *prophecy*.[10]

LETTER

It might be surprising to hear, but Revelation is a letter and *not* a book in the modern sense of that word.[11] Growing up, I never paid much attention to this fact. Yet, it is right there in the text: "John to the seven churches that are in Asia: Grace to you and peace from him who is and who was and who is to come" (Rev 1:4).[12] John follows the standard letter-writing format of his day: he begins with the sender's

---

10. Revelation has rightly been called "a *hybrid* document," that is, "it seems to possess features of several literary forms" (Gorman, *Reading Revelation*, 13; see also 29). In addition to letter, apocalypse, and prophecy, Gorman highlights two other literary aspects of Revelation, namely, its liturgical and political aspects (13). In this chapter I will discuss the first three of these, and in the next I will discuss the political aspect.

11. It is true that Revelation also refers to itself as a "book" (*biblion, biblos*; Rev 1:11). However, it would be anachronistic to read into this the idea of a modern-day, published book. A book in the modern sense is not associated with personalized letter-writing. It does not seek to take into account its reader's specific, individual concerns in a personalized sort of way. On Revelation as a letter, see Richard Bauckham, *The Theology of the Book of Revelation*, NTT (Cambridge: Cambridge University Press, 1993), 12–17.

12. For discussion of the identity of the author, see Ben Witherington, *Revelation*, NCBC (New York: Cambridge University Press, 2003), 1–10; Wright and Bird, *New Testament in Its World*, 812–14; Keener, *Revelation*, 54–55; Colin J. Hemer, *The Letters to the Seven Churches of Asia in Their Local Setting* (Grand Rapids: Eerdmans, 1989), 2–3; Gorman, *Reading Revelation*, 27–28.

name, followed by naming the recipients and offering a greeting.[13] This resembles what we see in other New Testament letters (see, e.g., Rom 1:1–7; 1 Cor 1:1–2; 2 Cor 1:1).

The letter is sent to seven different congregations. Each of these churches existed in a city in the Roman province of Asia, which is the western part of modern-day Turkey: Ephesus, Smyrna, Pergamum, Thyatira, Sardis, Philadelphia, and Laodicea (Rev 1:11).[14] The first three chapters of Revelation contain individual messages to each of these churches. For example, John is told to send a specific message to the church at Ephesus (Rev 2:1–7), to Smyrna's church (2:8–11), and so on. Each church, located as it was in a different city, was given instructions and encouragement that spoke directly to them and their situation.[15] The entirety of Revelation (including chapters 4–22) was given to these seven churches for their edification, with other churches in the region no doubt hearing about and benefiting from the message as well.[16] These churches appear to have been in great need of spiritual encouragement and guidance due to the trials and tribulations they were experiencing. Notice, for example, what John says at the beginning of his letter: "I, John, your brother and partner in the tribulation and the kingdom and the patient endurance that are in Jesus" (Rev 1:9a).

That John did not have to explain who he was (other than provide his name) indicates John was no stranger to the seven churches, and he most likely already had an established relationship with them.[17] He describes himself as their "brother" and "partner" (Rev

---

13. David A. deSilva, *Discovering Revelation: Content, Interpretation, Reception*, DBT (Grand Rapids: Eerdmans, 2021), 17.

14. On the Roman provincial system, especially with respect to Asia, see deSilva, *Discovering Revelation*, 52–53.

15. Pergamum (Rev 2:12–17), Thyatira (2:18–29), Sardis (3:1–6), Philadelphia (3:7–13), Laodicea (3:14–22).

16. Keener, *Revelation*, 67–68. Keener says, "Churches had spread throughout the province of Asia and were not limited to the cities mentioned in Revelation (Acts 19:10). But John writes to the most prominent and strategic seven cities in the region, from which word would quickly spread to outlying areas" (67). See also Steven J. Friesen, *Imperial Cults and the Apocalypse of John: Reading Revelation in the Ruins* (New York: Oxford University Press, 2001), 136, 180.

17. See the discussion in Witherington, *Revelation*, 9; Gorman, *Reading Revelation*, 27.

1:9). Christians commonly viewed each other as brothers and sisters, members of the same family of God, regardless of whether they knew each other well (a common practice among believers even today). But the fact that John also describes himself as a "partner" is significant. This suggests that John knew about and was a participant in these churches' specific hardships and their tribulation.[18]

These churches were undergoing persecution, testing, and trial—or, at the very least, they were undergoing *threats* of these things.[19] We know, for example, that at the church in Pergamum, one Christian had been recently martyred for his faith (Rev 2:13). Likewise, the church at Smyrna is told persecution awaits them and that they must be "faithful unto death" (2:10). Interestingly, Philadelphia's church is told it will be spared from the upcoming trial that awaits "the whole world" (3:10). Some of these churches do in fact exhibit "patient endurance" during persecution, showing faithfulness to Christ and his truth despite temptations to do otherwise (e.g., 2:2; 3:10). Others, however, have room for growth in this area and are currently compromising and need to repent (e.g., 2:19–20; 3:15–18).

By describing himself as a "partner" with these churches in their "tribulation" and in the "patient endurance" (Rev 1:9), John conveys a personal awareness of these churches' struggles.[20] He certainly knows what they are going through, and he is in effect saying, "I'm with you in the struggle." It makes sense that he would be familiar with their trials given that he was on the island of Patmos, which was not far from the city of Ephesus. In fact, it could have been the case that, prior to his exile, he had served as a leader in one of these churches.[21]

---

18. On John's situation and relation to Asia, see Witherington, *Revelation*, 78–80; Keener, *Revelation*, 81–83. See also Bauckham, *Revelation*, 13; Gorman, *Reading Revelation*, 27, 31–32.

19. Scholars debate what sort of persecutions were going on (and when). For a brief overview of the various views, as well as their implications for the dating of Revelation, see Friesen, *Imperial Cults*, 143–45. See also Alan S. Bandy, "Persecution and the Purpose of Revelation with Reference to Roman Jurisprudence," *BBR* 23 (2013): 377–98.

20. See Hemer, *Letters to the Seven Churches*, 2–3.

21. Witherington, *Revelation*, 9. See also Hemer, *Letters to the Seven Churches*, 27–29; Gorman, *Reading Revelation*, 27.

These observations show how Revelation was a personal letter that spoke to the unique situations of the seven churches. This brings us to an important point: Revelation, as a letter, must have been written so that it could be understood by its recipients. Otherwise, what would have been the point of writing a letter? It is unlikely that John wrote a letter he did not want his readers to understand. For starters, the text itself states the goal is to gain understanding. John says, "Blessed is the one who reads aloud the words of this prophecy, and blessed are those who hear, and who keep what is written in it, for the time is near" (Rev 1:3).

In the first century, people wrote letters and sent them via a letter carrier. In the case of Revelation, the letter carrier most likely took the entire letter to each church one at a time. Upon arriving at the church, either the letter carrier or a local church leader would have read the message out loud to the congregation.[22] One reason for this, perhaps, is that most people during this period of history were illiterate. It makes sense, then, that John pronounces blessings on both the reader *and* the hearers. When you look closely at Revelation 1:3, quoted above, you will notice that the reader is written in the singular ("the one who reads") while the hearers are in the plural ("those who hear").

John expects these congregations to listen closely to all he has to say. But he wants his readers to do more than listen. He wants them to obey. In the Hebrew tradition, hearing always conveyed the idea of obeying. Craig Keener notes this fact and also points out that "John allows no ambiguity" in what he wants his recipients to do—he wants them to "keep" the message, that is, to live a life of obedience in light of John's message.[23] The blessing is for those "who hear, *and who keep* what is written in it" (Rev 1:3, emphasis added). But John's original

---

22. Grant R. Osborne, *Revelation: Verse by Verse*, ONTC (Bellingham, WA: Lexham Press, 2016), 22.

23. Keener, *Revelation*, 56. The word used here is *tēreō*, and here it means "to obey," following closely the commands one receives (compare Keener, *Revelation*, 56–57). Says deSilva: "John ... intended his letter to be understood by *them*, to shape *their* perceptions of *their* everyday realities, and to motivate a particular response to *their* circumstances" (*Unholy Allegiances*, 3, emphasis original).

readers could only obey the message of Revelation if the details of that letter spoke directly to their time. In order for the letter to be *obeyable* it first had to be *understandable*.[24]

This makes sense because Revelation is all about helping readers to understand truth, not confusing them. Notice the opening lines of Revelation: "The revelation of Jesus Christ" (Rev 1:1). The word translated as "revelation" is *apokalypsis*, which is where we get our modern word "apocalypse." Unfortunately, that word is now loaded with associations with doomsday, world wars, and nuclear annihilation. But none of these accurately describe the term.

"Apocalypse" simply means "that which is unveiled" or "unconcealed." This gives us a strong clue about the intention and purpose of John's letter: Revelation is meant to shed light on something important for its readers, not cover anything up. Revelation's goal is to clarify the nature of reality, not wrap it up in a blanket of obscurity. As David deSilva says,

> Revelation was not sent to those seven churches as a mysterious text needing to *be* interpreted: it was sent to *interpret* the world of those readers. To put this another way, the first readers and hearers did not need a special "key" to unlock Revelation; Revelation *was* the key by which they could unlock the real meaning of what was going on around them, and so respond to it faithfully.[25]

---

24. So Keener: "If we take seriously what the book itself *claims*, then it was a book that must have made good sense to its first hearers, who in fact were 'blessed' for obeying it (1:3). That John wrote the book in Greek probably suggests that he also used figures of speech and symbols that were part of his culture more than ours. That the book was to remain 'unsealed' even in his generation also indicates that it was meant to be understood from that time forward (22:10; contrast Dan. 12:9–10)" (*Revelation*, 21, emphasis original). Elsewhere, Keener asks, "Were the original readers of the book of Revelation expected to be able to understand it?" He answers this in the affirmative, citing Rev 1:3, which makes it clear that "we are expected to obey its message, which presumably means we are expected to understand its message, at least well enough to live accordingly." See Craig Keener, "Understanding Revelation," YouTube, June 5, 2017, https://youtu.be/BIJRlQhWi5w.

25. DeSilva, *Unholy Allegiances*, 8, emphasis original; see also Gorman, *Reading Revelation*, 22.

So, Revelation, as a personal letter, must have been understandable to its original hearers. Otherwise, it could not have spoken directly to their own challenging times—to their difficulties, their hardships, their sufferings.

These observations serve as yet another caution to those who insist Revelation is all about the future. The truth is that Revelation was a first-century letter that encouraged its original readers to obey— to live out and apply—its truths in their own context. Hence, the message of Revelation dealt largely with issues and topics going on at that time (the first century) and at that place (Asia Minor). It was written *to them.* And before we can get to any modern-day application *for us,* we first need to learn about Revelation's original context—the world of its recipients and the challenges they faced. Because Revelation is an ancient, personal letter to the first-century churches of Asia Minor, we need to read it on their terms. If we don't, our modern applications will get off on the wrong foot.

APOCALYPSE

We've discussed how Revelation is a letter, but it also falls under the category of apocalyptic literature. Around the time John was writing his own apocalypse, there were other apocalypses in circulation. One of them was 1 Enoch, which is an intriguing book on a number of levels. It includes, for example, an ancient story about rogue spiritual beings who had sexual relations with women and taught people how to kill each other more effectively (not my first pick for nighttime reading). The point was to offer Jews a sort of behind-the-scenes look at events that took place in Genesis 6, revealing an otherwise hidden perspective about them. As I mentioned above this is why it is called an apocalypse—it was meant to unveil what was really going on.[26]

Scholars go back and forth on how exactly to define and understand the apocalyptic genre, and it's a matter of ongoing conversation.[27]

---

26. There are, of course, other writings that fall broadly under the genre "apocalyptic literature." For a helpful resource, see *OTP* 1.

27. To familiarize yourself with the issues, I recommend reading John J. Collins, "Introduction: Towards the Morphology of a Genre," *Semeia* 14 (1979): 9; Bauckham, *Revelation,*

But for our purposes, here is a simplified working description: *an apoc-alypse seeks to challenge current perceptions about reality and reveal the truth about that reality from God's perspective.* Thus, according to deSilva,

> Apocalypses set an audience's space within the context of a larger, invisible world, and they set the audience's time in the context of a sacred history of God's activity and carefully defined plan. In so doing, they place the present moment and the challenges of the present situation in an interpretive frame-work, often explicitly evaluating and addressing those chal-lenges and that situation in light of that larger backdrop derived from the sacred tradition.[28]

Extensive use of symbols, metaphors, and vivid imagery is common in apocalypses. Visions can be another feature of apocalypses.[29] These elements evoke a sense of God's sovereignty over world events. In this way, apocalypses offer a "God's-eye view of history, the present, and the future."[30]

All of this is true of Revelation. Like every good apocalypse, Revelation employs symbolic language to communicate to its audi-ence. The point is to reveal God's truth in high definition. The enemies of God's people, for example, are depicted as beasts that come from the sea and the land (Rev 13). Revelation isn't warning the church to steer clear of Godzilla. It simply employs beastly imagery as a way to creatively communicate the inhumane and monstrous character of corrupt earthly powers, which in John's time was the Roman Empire (more on this later).

The key to interpreting apocalyptic literature is to keep this sort of symbolism in mind. Otherwise, we might fail to see all the wonder-ful truths Revelation has to offer. The power of symbolism is that it

---

5–12; Alan S. Bandy, *The Prophetic Lawsuit in the Book of Revelation*, NTM (Sheffield: Sheffield Phoenix, 2010), 1–3.

28. DeSilva, *Unholy Allegiances*, 9.

29. Gorman, *Reading Revelation*, 14.

30. Wright and Bird, *New Testament in Its World*, 824.

allows the writer to explain truth in a way that would otherwise evade normal language. It's a lot like going from two-dimensional drawings to three-dimensional prints; they are able to present an added layer of depth. Similarly, apocalyptic symbols add another dimension to what is communicated beyond what could be said in a typical letter. This allows readers to see their world in a fresh light. It peels back the curtain of physical reality, allowing them to get a glimpse of the spiritual realm. When we fail to account for Revelation's rich symbolism, we miss out on seeing the complete picture that God wants us to see. We miss out on the revealing of truth—God's *revelation*.

PROPHECY

Revelation isn't just a letter and an apocalypse; it is also prophetic. In fact, it is best understood as a "prophetic apocalypse or apocalyptic prophecy."[31] Scholar Richard Bauckham explains how these two work together, saying that Revelation

> is a prophetic apocalypse in that it communicates a disclosure of a transcendent perspective on this world. It is prophetic in the way it addresses a concrete historical situation—that of Christians in the Roman province of Asia towards the end of the first century AD—and brings to its readers a prophetic word of God, enabling them to discern the divine purpose in their situation and respond to their situation in a way appropriate to this purpose. ... But John's work is also *apocalyptic*, because the way that it enables its readers to see their situation with prophetic insight into God's purpose is by disclosing the content of a vision in which John is taken, as it were, out of this world in order to see it differently. ... He is given a glimpse behind the scenes of history so that he can see what is really going on in the events of his time and place.[32]

---

31. Bauckham, *Revelation*, 6.

32. Bauckham, *Revelation*, 7, emphasis original. See also 8–9 on how Revelation, as an apocalypse, reveals how God is the true Lord of the world and how it seeks to strengthen

In other words: the message of Revelation is meant to help believers in the seven churches gain an eternal and heavenly perspective about their life in first-century Asia Minor. As I said above, Revelation seeks to reveal the truth about their situation. It seeks to uncover the reality of their own trials and tribulations.

As an apocalypse, it reminds them who the true Lord and Savior of the world is. But as a prophetic word, it also calls the world to profess allegiance to this Lord. Revelation reveals truth to its readers, and it summons its readers to obey the truth. In this sense, Revelation is an invitation. It invites readers to forsake corrupt earthly allegiances and to hold fast to something better. This would have been an important message for the original readers of Revelation to hear. To find out why, we need to take a deeper look at the historical context.

STEP 2: KNOW THE HISTORICAL CONTEXT

Looking into the historical context of the seven churches makes perfect sense given that Revelation is a *letter*. The circumstances that gave rise to the letter itself are part of the letter's context. This context gives the letter its meaning. If you understand the historical *context* of the letter, you will be in a better position to understand the *contents* of the letter. This is interpretation 101.

When we pay close attention to what the letter of Revelation has to say, we immediately notice that the letter practically begs readers to take its historical setting seriously. An example of this can be seen in a passage we looked at previously, Revelation 1:9: "I, John, your brother and partner in the tribulation and the kingdom and the patient endurance that are in Jesus, was on the island called Patmos on account of the word of God and the testimony of Jesus."

Notice again how John describes himself: *your brother and partner in the tribulation.* Who is the "your"? The seven churches. According to John, he and the churches are living in troubled times. They are

---

believers' faith in this fact.

not merely spectators to the times; they are active participants. This is obvious due to how John describes himself as a partner in "the patient endurance ... in Jesus." The words "patient endurance" suggest that both he and his readers were, at the time of writing, undergoing some sort of persecution, or at least the threat of it. This makes sense in light of how the churches at Ephesus, Thyatira, and Philadelphia are all explicitly commended for their "patient endurance" (Rev 2:2, 19; 3:10). This also makes sense of John's statement that he was on Patmos "on account of the word of God and the testimony of Jesus." Perhaps John had fled to the island for safety or had been banished there by Rome as a punishment for preaching the gospel.[33] The latter is most likely the case.[34]

Apparently, Christians in this area had undergone persecutions before the letter was written as well. At Pergamum, for example, a believer named Antipas had been martyred for the faith (Rev 2:13). Similarly, Smyrna is commanded to stay faithful to Jesus because some of them will soon be imprisoned for their faith (2:10).

It was not just persecution the churches are experiencing, though. They were also experiencing temptation. For example, false teachers had apparently infiltrated the church at Pergamum and were leading people astray by permitting them to eat food dedicated to pagan idols and to engage in sexual immorality (Rev 2:14–15). Similarly, a false prophetess was leading believers to do the same thing in Thyatira (2:20). Christians in Philadelphia were also experiencing persecution, though not by the hands of pagans; it was from the Jewish synagogue (3:9).

These passages raise several questions. What was the situation surrounding Antipas' martyrdom? Why were Christians going to be imprisoned in Smyrna? What was going on with Christians being tempted to eat food dedicated to pagan idols? What events motivated

---

33. Friesen, *Imperial Cults*, 136.

34. Bandy, "Persecution and the Purpose of Revelation," 381–83. See also Gorman, *Reading Revelation*, 32.

Jews in Philadelphia to persecute followers of Christ? These are good, historically focused questions. Because they deal with the historical circumstances of the churches, we must embark on historical research in order to answer them. In other words, we need to go back in time and learn what it was like to live in the seven cities of the seven churches.

In the pages that follow, we will explore what life was like for our Christian brothers and sisters living in Asia Minor in the first century. We will survey their social, political, and religious context. This will help us to see that, for the original readers, the message of Revelation had less to do with future speculation and more to do with helping them find hope, comfort, and encouragement in the midst of their trials. The more we understand Revelation's historical context, the better we will be at applying its message to our present context.

REVELATION'S HISTORICAL CONTEXT

Living in the Roman Empire in the first century would have been difficult, especially if you were a Christian. While it is true that around the time Revelation was written (about AD 95) there had been no official empire-wide persecution of the church, there certainly had already been pockets of severe, periodic persecution in various places.[35]

One example comes from Tacitus, the well-known Roman historian. In his *Annals*, he tells how Emperor Nero (who reigned before Revelation was written) needed someone to blame for the burning of Rome. He found it convenient to lay the blame on Christians. As a result, many believers were subjected to death in the most heinous of tortures, such as being turned into human candles to light up Nero's garden at night (*Annals* 15.44).[36]

---

35. On the date of Revelation's writing, see Gorman, *Reading Revelation*, 28; deSilva, *Discovering Revelation*, 35–39; Grant R. Osborne, *Revelation*, BECNT (Grand Rapids: Baker, 2002), 6–9.

36. Tacitus, *The Annals*, Oxford translation, revised, Bohn's Classical Library (London: Henry G. Bohn, 1854), 1:422–23. Unless otherwise indicated, all quotations from *The Annals* are taken from this edition.

This persecution, while horrific, was not permanent or official empire-wide policy. It was the result of the spasmodic insanity of Nero.[37] This particular season of persecution was most likely limited to the city of Rome, and it seemed to have stopped once Nero was finished with his madness.[38] But with that said, for first-century Christians living in Asia, the threat of persecution always lingered in the air.[39] And sometimes the threat would become a reality.

WORSHIPING THE EMPEROR

If we want to understand what it was like for Christians living in Asia—and in all parts of the Roman Empire—we need to know a thing or two about how people viewed the emperor in the first century.[40] By the time Revelation was written, it had become customary for Roman emperors to be deified after they died, becoming "gods" for Roman citizens to worship. For instance, after Julius Caesar died, he was treated as a god, and his adopted son, Octavius, took the title "son of god."[41] Such titles were meant to elevate the emperor, linking him with the established pantheon of gods and goddesses. This helped to legitimate his rule.

Though it was common by the end of the first century that an emperor would be worshiped as a god *after* he died, the Greek-speaking population of Asia Minor had a habit of jumping the gun; they would worship the Roman emperor while he was still alive.[42]

---

37. See also Bandy, "Persecution and the Purpose of Revelation," 379, who says, "Overall, the persecution of Christians in Asia Minor for the first two centuries is best characterized as local and sporadic"; see also 387.

38. On Nero's persecution being local to Rome, see Witherington, *Revelation*, 4. On the "short lived" nature of this persecution, see Bandy, "Persecution and the Purpose of Revelation," 397–98 (see also 391n83).

39. See Bandy, "Persecution and the Purpose of Revelation," esp. 377–80.

40. This section is a revision of Matthew L. Halsted, "The Covid Vaccine Has 666 Written All over It ... and Why That Doesn't Matter According to Revelation," *The Logos Academic Blog*, May 18, 2020.

41. Floyd O. Parker, "'Our Lord and God' in Rev 4,11: Evidence for the Late Date of Revelation," *Biblica* 82 (2001): 213–14.

42. For a good introduction to emperor worship in Asia, see J. Nelson Kraybill, *Apocalypse and Allegiance: Worship, Politics, and Devotion in the Book of Revelation* (Grand Rapids: Brazos, 2010), 53–70.

Living emperors were often described with a variety of titles such as "savior," "god," and "lord."[43]

Take Caesar Augustus, for instance. In an inscription from Asia Minor that predates the birth of Christ, we read how Augustus was hailed as a "savior" and as a "god," and his birth was even proclaimed as *good news* (literally, "gospel") to the world.[44] For many people living in Asia Minor, Augustus was esteemed as the divine answer to the problems of the world—while he was still alive.[45]

For Romans, worshiping a deceased emperor was permissible, but to worship an emperor while he was still alive was outside accepted norms. For Greeks, however, the practice of worshiping political leaders as gods was not all that unusual. When compared to the Greeks, Craig Keener writes,

> Most Romans themselves were far more restrained; they recognized that the emperor was a mortal and could be made a god only after death (an act that required senate approval). To claim deity while still alive in Rome itself was considered an act of hubris, of supreme arrogance, and usually resulted in the cursing of the emperor's name after death. ... In the eastern Mediterranean, however, most peoples showed their loyalty to Rome by worshiping not only the goddess Roma (Rome) but also the emperor.[46]

Why didn't the Romans discourage the Greeks from doing this? Their reasoning was in many ways practical. This phenomenon (what scholars call "the imperial cult") was politically advantageous for everyone involved—for Caesar and the Asian cities that participated

---

43. See the helpful catalog of titles for various emperors in Parker, "'Our Lord and God,'" 213–17.

44. F. Frhr. Hiller von Gaertringen, ed., *Inschriften von Priene* (Berlin: Reimer, 1906), 105.35–41 (my translation). For a good translation of and discussion about the inscription, see Friesen, *Imperial Cults*, 32–36. See also Kraybill, *Apocalypse and Allegiance*, 56–57.

45. See the discussion in deSilva, *Unholy Allegiances*, 25–27.

46. Keener, *Revelation*, 37.

in it.[47] For Caesar, it was good for patriotism, fostering allegiance to the empire. For the cities, it helped earn points with Caesar to gain access to things such as economic and military assistance when they needed it.[48]

This probably sounds strange to us in the modern world, where we tend to keep politics and religion separate. But this was not so for people living in the first century. To Roman citizens, the two were deeply connected. And in places such as Asia, paying homage to gods (such as the emperor) would have been at times a prerequisite for maintaining any sort of sociopolitical or economic identity and reputation. Politics and religion were mutually supporting.[49] And the imperial cult wasn't just something people invented to serve political ends. In fact, "the imperial cult ... was much more than a mere political tool; participants actually worshiped the emperor as divine."[50] So, we should not fail to see the religious side of things. In the first century, religion was political, and politics were religious.

All of this is important information for how we understand the churches of Revelation and Revelation itself. Scholars have pointed out that the worship of emperors was happening throughout the province of Asia, where John sent his letter.[51]

CITIES IN COMPETITION

How did cities become centers for the worship of the emperor? The leaders of Asia, in conversation with the Roman senate and the emperor, chose cities within their region to serve as hosts for imperial cult temples.

---

47. On "the cult of the Roman emperors and the goddess Roma," see deSilva, *Discovering Revelation*, 47–50. See also the numerous sources cited below.

48. DeSilva, *Unholy Allegiances*, 29.

49. See deSilva, *Discovering Revelation*, 45–46.

50. Bandy, "Persecution and the Purpose of Revelation," 393.

51. Parker, "'Our Lord and God,'" 213–14. See also Tae Hun Kim, "The Anarthrous υἱὸς θεοῦ in Mark 15,39 and the Roman Imperial Cult," *Biblica* 79 (1998): 221–41; Mark Wilson, "The Early Christians in Ephesus and the Date of Revelation, Again," *Neotestamentica* 39 (2005): 171; Duane Warden, "Imperial Persecution and the Dating of 1 Peter and Revelation," *JETS* 34 (June 1991): 211; Keener, *Revelation*, 37–38.

An entire worship system was established. There were priests, altars, feasts, sacrifices, and, of course, temples set up in various cities through-out Asia so that citizens could express their devotion to Rome by wor-shiping Caesar and his family.[52] Asia was enmeshed in the imperial cult—it was part of its DNA. In fact, the cities of Asia often competed with one another to become locations for provincial imperial cult temples.

Pergamum was the first city in Asia to build a provincial temple for the worship of Augustus (along with the goddess Roma) in 29 BC. Later, Smyrna and Sardis vied to become the site of a second temple, with Smyrna being awarded the prize in AD 26. Several decades later, just prior to the writing of Revelation, Ephesus became the site of a third provincial temple to the emperor (AD 89/90). In addition to this, there's also evidence to suggest Asia Minor was home "to more than 80 smaller localized imperial temples in more than 60 cities."[53] I want to explain a little bit more about this to give an idea of the sort of world the Christians of the area were living in.

When a city was granted an imperial provincial temple, it became known as a *Neokoros*. This word means "temple warden," and over time, it became a "title of honor," one that Asian cities lobbied hard to acquire.[54] I can't emphasize just how important the title *Neokoros* became for Asian cities. Obtaining the title would become the focus of intense competition between them. In fact, by the time John sent his letter to the seven churches in the mid-90s, the title *Neokoros* had become "the most prestigious self-designation that could be employed by a city in Asia."[55]

As I mentioned, Pergamum was the first to receive a provincial imperial temple. This was a *provincial* temple, that is, one that was sponsored by the entire province of Asia. Thus, the worship of the

---

52. For an excellent overview of this phenomenon in Asia, see Friesen, *Imperial Cults*, 23–131.

53. Bandy, "Persecution and the Purpose of Revelation," 392–93 (see also for cities and dates mentioned above). See also Friesen, *Imperial Cults*, 23–55.

54. DeSilva, *Unholy Allegiances*, 28, and Friesen, *Imperial Cults*, 47–50, 55, respectively. See also deSilva, *Discovering Revelation*, 48–50.

55. Friesen, *Imperial Cults*, 150.

emperor was not a localized phenomenon in just one city. Far from it. The temple rituals and worship would have had the support of all citizens of Asia—except, of course, for faithful Christians, who would never have worshiped Caesar as god. We know that this was exactly what was happening in Pergamum from an inscription found there. The inscription describes Augustus as a *theos*, "god."[56] For Christians living in Pergamum, to see a temple dedicated to the worship of Caesar as "god" would have been the epitome of blasphemy. Could this be why in Revelation Jesus describes Pergamum as the place where "Satan's throne" is and where Satan himself lives (Rev 2:13)? Perhaps so, though later in this chapter we will see two other reasons why Pergamum might have been identified as the place where Satan lived.

Like I mentioned earlier, Smyrna competed with Sardis in AD 26 to become the site of a second provincial temple, with Smyrna eventually coming out on top. The timing of this competition is rather ironic. While these pagan cities were vying to be the next location for the worship of Caesar, the true King was already on the scene in Judea, about to launch his world-altering ministry.

Before the first century came to a close, a third provincial temple was dedicated in Ephesus to the emperor Domitian and his family (AD 89/90). Domitian was prone to unusual violence. To give us but a sample of Domitian's sadistic heart, the historian Suetonius offers the following story: "Domitian was not merely cruel, but cunning and sudden into the bargain. He summoned a Palace steward to his bedroom, invited him to join him on his couch, made him feel perfectly secure and happy, condescended to share a dinner with him— yet had him crucified on the following day!" (*Dom.* 11).[57] Apparently, Domitian got a kick out of murder for the heck of it.

According to Suetonius, Domitian was also arrogant enough to insist on going by the title "Lord and God" (*Dom.* 13). Because of this and other things, says Suetonius, Domitian was "everywhere

---

56. Friesen, *Imperial Cults*, 31.

57. All references to *The Twelve Caesars* are taken from Suetonius, *The Twelve Caesars*, trans. Robert Graves, rev. Michael Grant (New York: Penguin Books, 2003).

hated and feared" (*Dom.* 14). I tend to agree with those who think John wrote Revelation around AD 95, which was when Domitian was the emperor.[58] It is helpful to remember, too, that one of the seven churches to whom John wrote—namely, Ephesus—was a recent recipient of a provincial temple for the worship of Domitian and his family. Suffice it to say, the Christians of Asia were not living in paradise under a benevolent ruler. To the contrary, the Roman Empire was led by a man of beastly intentions.

This was the world of Christians living in Asia Minor, and it would have been a difficult life. No doubt they needed encouragement, hope, and comfort. They needed to know that, despite what they were seeing and hearing, there was a greater reality at work. They needed to be reminded that one day the Lamb would conquer the Beast. In other words, *they needed an apocalypse.* That's why John sent them a letter.

Many New Testament scholars think Revelation was a commentary on the empire and the imperial cult. As Michael Gorman says, "Nearly all interpreters of Revelation recognize that the entire book is a critique and parody of the Roman Empire and of the cult of the emperor that was rampant in the Roman province of Asia in the second half of the first century."[59] The point of Revelation was to *reveal* a different sort of kingdom, a different sort of politics. It will do the same for our world today if we have ears to hear.

A GALORE OF PAGAN CULTS

As important as the imperial cult was to the Roman Empire in general and to Asia in particular, it was not the only cult that enjoyed devotion from citizens. In fact, it was just one among many. "The dominant culture was awash in Greco-Roman religions with its plethora of gods, goddesses, and temples," Alan Bandy writes.[60] Asia was littered with all sorts of shrines and temples to various deities. Take Ephesus, for

---

58. See again Gorman, who thinks "a date for Revelation toward the end of Domitian's reign seems most likely" (*Reading Revelation*, 28).

59. Gorman, *Reading Revelation*, 40.

60. Bandy, "Persecution and the Purpose of Revelation," 392.

example. The temple to the Greek goddess Artemis was there, and it was quite the sight. The temple was so magnificent that it was considered one of the ancient wonders of the world. Artemis was the goddess of fertility, and Ephesus was regarded as the custodian of the cult itself (see Acts 19:35).[61] Devotion to her was paramount for people living in Ephesus.

We can see an example of how the Artemis cult was fused into the very lifeblood of Ephesus from an event that takes place in Acts 19. There, we read how Paul and his fellow ministry workers traveled to Ephesus to share the gospel. Their ministry causes quite the stir; in fact, when Christianity (known then as "the Way") is introduced to Ephesus, a riot ensues:

> About that time there arose no little disturbance concerning the Way. For a man named Demetrius, a silversmith, who made silver shrines of Artemis, brought no little business to the craftsmen. These he gathered together, with the workmen in similar trades, and said, "Men, you know that from this business we have our wealth. And you see and hear that not only in Ephesus but in almost all of Asia this Paul has persuaded and turned away a great many people, saying that gods made with hands are not gods. And there is danger not only that this trade of ours may come into disrepute but also that the temple of the great goddess Artemis may be counted as nothing, and that she may even be deposed from her magnificence, she whom all Asia and the world worship." When they heard this they were enraged and were crying out, "Great is Artemis of the Ephesians!" (Acts 19:23–27)

As a result, the city of Ephesus is "filled with the confusion," and Paul's fellow ministers are brought before the rioting crowd, presumably to

---

61. On Artemis, her temple, her cult, and her place and function in Ephesus, see Wright and Bird, *New Testament in Its World*, 156, 356, 453, 455–57. On Artemis being the "divine guardian and benefactor of the city" of Ephesus, see 456. See also deSilva, *Discovering Revelation*, 46.

give an account of what they are doing (19:29). After some time passes, the town clerk finally succeeds in calming everyone down before they cause too much trouble (19:35–41).

In places such as Asia, pagan cults such as the Artemis cult were very important to public life. An example of this can be seen in a yearly ritual that was performed when the large seaport at Ephesus was opened. Artemis's priests took her statue and ceremonially placed it "into the water as a sign of her blessing upon the merchant vessels that brought prosperity to the city and as a symbol of her protection upon the vessels' sailors during the following year."[62] Any threat to the pagan cult (whether real or perceived) was interpreted as a threat to people's way of life—not least to their economic way of life. There was big money to be made, and local economies were often situated around pagan cults. We can see this also in how Demetrius was able to gather around him other tradesmen whose own livelihoods depended, on some level, on the Artemis cult (19:25).[63]

Other gods and goddesses were venerated in Ephesus, too. One such goddess was Hestia Boulaia. A flame to her honor was lit on the grounds of an important government building, the Prytaneion. She occupied a prime place in the life of Ephesians:

> As goddess of fire and the family hearth she became, by extension, goddess of the family unit and of the broader family, the civic community. A sanctuary in her honor was maintained on the premises, and a priesthood existed to ensure that the fire never went out. Since Artemis was patron goddess of the city, her statue was also found in the Prytaneion and there was considerable overlap in personnel between those who serve the two goddesses.[64]

In addition to Hestia, a plethora of other gods and goddesses were venerated and worshiped in the ancient city of Ephesus: Aphrodite,

---

62. Roland H. Worth Jr., *The Seven Cities of the Apocalypse and Greco-Asian Culture* (Mahwah, NJ: Paulist, 1999), 17.

63. On the various trade guilds in Ephesus, see Worth, *Seven Cities*, 29.

64. Worth, *Seven Cities*, 24.

Athena, Demeter, Cybele, Asclepius, Apollo, Dionysus, Isis, and Serapis—to name a few.[65]

Pagan cults also flourished in Pergamum, another of the cities to which John wrote Revelation. Pergamum's "four most important cults" were those of Zeus, Dionysus, Asclepius, and Athena.[66] This city was well-known for its altar to Zeus, who was a very important figure in the Greek pantheon. It would be no stretch of the imagination, then, to say that this altar would have had a fair amount of traffic from zealous devotees.

Pergamum was also home to a temple dedicated to Asclepius.[67] In the ancient world, Asclepius was the god of healing and medicine, and his temple (known as an Asclepeion) was a place the sick and ailing could go to find healing. Asclepius was commonly associated with serpents, and he was often depicted with a staff that had a serpent wrapped around it. Modern Americans might be familiar with this, as it is similar to the symbol adopted by the American Medical Association.[68] If a person were sick or had any sort of debilitating ailment, they could spend a few nights in rooms in the Asclepeion. There the sick would receive dreams from the god on how they could be healed—divine prescriptions of sorts. These dreams prescribed various solutions to illnesses, from strenuous physical activity to baths to drinking liquid concoctions made from snakes.[69]

Some scholars think it is possible that Revelation 2:13—which refers to "Satan's throne" being in Pergamum—might be a reference to Asclepius's temple. This may very well be the case, since early Christians associated Satan with a serpent. It is also possible that

---

65. Worth, *Seven Cities*, 48–50.

66. Worth, *Seven Cities*, 112.

67. For a good overview on the cult of Asclepius, see Robin Thompson, "Healing at the Pool of Bethesda: A Challenge to Asclepius?," *BBR* 27 (2017): 77–79; Worth, *Seven Cities*, 116–22.

68. See Thompson, "Healing at the Pool," 77n92, where he notes that whereas the American Medical Association depicts a staff with two snakes wrapped around it, Asclepius's has but one snake.

69. Worth, *Seven Cities*, 117, 120–21.

it refers to the altar to Zeus, the imperial cult, or something else.[70] Whatever the case, we can know for sure that the church in Pergamum was being attacked by Satan on a number of fronts.

The worship of gods and goddesses was not a thing ancient people did for a couple of hours on one day a week (they were much more devoted than many modern Christians!). To them, the gods infused every aspect of daily life. From work to feasts to medicine, the gods were everywhere, lurking behind every nook and cranny of social and political life.

If you were a Christian living in one of these cities, you would have had to navigate this minefield of allegiances to other gods in your personal and professional life. Christians could not in good conscience take part in the feasts or economic partnerships (trade guilds) that were centered on pagan gods and goddesses. They could not give allegiance to Caesar, nor worship him as a god or son of a god. This would have been out of the question. Christians were committed to the worship of Jesus only, not to the idols of their culture. Refusing to worship Caesar was costly. It would have at times meant certain death for Christians. Living for Jesus would have been a life lived on the margins of society—as social outcasts and a persecuted minority.

SUMMING UP

Life in first-century Asia Minor was thoroughly pagan. The gods were everywhere. Temples and shrines peppered the landscape. Food was dedicated to the gods, and prayers were uttered to the gods. For Christians, all of this would have been difficult to tiptoe around. There were temptations to compromise, to go back to an easier way of life.

---

70. See the discussion in David E. Aune, *Revelation 1–5*, WBC (Dallas: Word, 1997), 182–84. Aune mentions the imperial cult as a candidate, which I think is very likely, too. In total, he lists eight possible references—all of which have some merit (see 182–83). In the end, he concludes that the reference to "Satan's throne" should not be taken as a reference to any "specific architectural feature of Roman Pergamum" but is, rather, to be taken more generally as "*Roman opposition* to early Christianity" (183–84, emphasis original).

As Jesus followers, they could not have participated in pagan feasts or in the worship of Caesar. In a world where this was not only normal but expected, Christians would have been easily noticed and called out. To faithful Roman citizens, Christians would have appeared weird and even deviant. That's because, quite frankly, they were. As exiles, all Christians live away from their true home. As people of the cross, we today can even appear quite deviant when compared to those who choose to endorse the policies of empire.

Because the first Christians were countercultural in nearly every respect, their beliefs would have been understood as a challenge to the politics of Rome. Christianity was not just another worship system that could exist side-by-side with the pagan cults. To the contrary, Christians were proclaiming a rival message. They were challenging Caesar's claim to be the savior of the world. By proclaiming the *good news* of Jesus as Savior and Lord, the early Christians were saying Caesar was not the hope of the world. Jesus's birth was gospel, not Caesar's. Jesus's enemy-loving, cross-bearing ways were completely antithetical to Caesar's enemy-hating, cross-killing ways.

It is no wonder, then, that Revelation opens with John talking about being a "partner" in the trials and tribulations of the seven churches. We can now see why Jesus would exhort the churches to stay faithful to him, warning them specifically not to participate in idol worship and not to tolerate people who taught them to do so.

As I said at the beginning of the chapter, the *context* of Revelation allows us to understand the *content* of Revelation. Now we can see why Revelation says what it does. And perhaps even already you have begun to connect the dots:

- As a letter, Revelation was written to seven real churches, which implies that its message was understandable to its original readers. As an apocalypse, Revelation uses symbolic language to reveal a God's-eye perspective for the encouragement of Christians living in Caesar's empire. And as a prophecy, Revelation warns the churches

against idolatry (Rev 2:14–15). This makes sense given
how idols and temples peppered the Asian landscape.

- Revelation encourages Christians to remain faithful in
  trials (Rev 2:10, 13). It's no wonder that Revelation would
  include this, as the threat of persecution was constant.

- Revelation tells the story of how Satan has inspired an
  evil, beastly kingdom but that one day the Lamb will
  rescue the world from it (Rev 12–13; 17–22). That such
  a story is included is not at all surprising given that the
  message of the idolatrous empire was etched on every
  official document and ingrained on every temple.

- Revelation identifies two groups of people who have
  been marked out as either Lamb people or Beast people
  (Rev 7; 13–14). This makes perfect sense because, in the
  first century, there was only one choice: pledge loyalty
  to either Christ or Caesar.

All of this helps us begin to see that it's probably a mistake to think
Revelation's message is all about the future. It is perhaps better to see
Revelation as a timeless message for every era and not just an outline of events for the final generation. Instead of looking out for just a
future Beast, for example, every Christian throughout history should
be conscious of the beastly systems already present. Remember, *we*
are living in the end times, as every Christian has for the past two
thousand years. And like those living in the first century, we in the
twenty-first have the same choice to make: Will we bear the mark of
the Lamb or the mark of the Beast? That's not just a question for the
future, but also one for *today*.

3

WHAT IS THE MARK
OF THE BEAST?

I f there's one passage in Revelation that is most well-known, it would probably be the one that refers to the mark of the Beast, with its intriguing mention of the number 666 (Rev 13:16–18). Through the years, countless theories have made the rounds about what it might mean. When President Reagan was alive, for example, some speculated it might refer to him. Each of his three names, after all, contains exactly six letters: Ronald Wilson Reagan (hence 666). Because Revelation speaks of the mark of the Beast as being a way to "buy or sell" (Rev 13:17), some have worried the mark was a barcode (perhaps it was secretly coded with "666"). Social Security numbers and credit cards have also been a concern for the same reason (in case three sixes appeared together). Today, speculative theories tend to center on microchips and nanotechnology. It seems that as technology develops, so does the speculation. During the Covid-19 pandemic, a lot of speculation circulated that suggested the vaccine for the virus might be the mark of the Beast.[1] All of this has led many sincere Christians into panic. Some have become quite fearful they might be tricked into accepting the mark without knowing it.

---

1. See, e.g., Scott Gleeson and Asha C. Gilbert, "Some Say COVID-19 Vaccine Is the 'Mark of the Beast.' Is There a Connection to the Bible?," *USA Today*, September 26, 2021, https://www.usatoday.com/story/news/nation/2021/09/26/covid-vaccine-mark -beast-what-book-revelation-says/8255268002/.

So what is the mark of the Beast? To answer that question, we need to remember something from the last chapter: *before we can understand the content of Revelation, we need to understand the context of Revelation.* Since Revelation was originally written as a letter, it must have held meaning for its original readers. In fact, John thought it was possible for his first-century audience to discern what the mark meant (Rev 13:18). He also comes out and says what the mark is: "the name of the beast or the number of its name" (13:17). Admittedly, this makes little sense to us modern people. How can a name also be a number? To answer this question, we need to think like a first-century Jew. But before we can identify *the mark* of the Beast, we first need to identify the Beast.

THE MARK OF THE ... WHO?

Revelation 13 mentions not just one but *two* beasts. The first is said to emerge "out of the sea" (Rev 13:1), and the second comes "out of the earth" (13:11). Both are empowered by a sinister dragon, who is identified as "that ancient serpent, who is called the devil and Satan, "the deceiver of the whole world" (12:9). The dragon empowers the beasts to "make war" on followers of Jesus (12:17).

The first Beast, from the sea, is a rather odd-looking creature. It is a seven-headed monster, decked out with ten horns. The heads are tattooed with "blasphemous names," and the horns are gilded with diadems (Rev 13:1). The Beast is described as a sort of mutant, animal hybrid. The Beast is "like a leopard," with bear's feet and a lion's mouth (13:2). One of its seven heads suffers from a "mortal wound." But remarkably, "its mortal wound was healed," which evokes praise and astonishment from "the whole earth" (13:3).

The Beast, like the dragon, becomes an object of worship: "And they worshiped the dragon, for he had given his authority to the beast, and they worshiped the beast, saying, 'Who is like the beast, and who can fight against it?' " (13:4). The text connects the concept of worship with the Beast's military prowess ("who can fight against it?"). The Beast is confessed to be second to none.

Remember from the previous chapter that first-century people did not divorce politics from worship. The two went together hand-in-glove. That's what is going on here. The Beast is a military—and hence political—figure who is worshiped. The Beast has both a throne and authority as well as an ability to "make war on the saints" (13:2, 5–7). The Beast's rage is directed against God and God's people. He has "a mouth uttering haughty and blasphemous words"—specifically "against God, blaspheming his name and his dwelling, that is, those who dwell in heaven" (13:6).

The second beast is intimately connected to the first Beast's menacing campaign of holy war. This beast also looks odd. He has two horns "like a lamb," though he speaks "like a dragon" (13:11). In other words, he looks innocent on the outside, but he is nefarious within. His mission is to make everyone worship the first Beast (13:12). He employs "great signs" to persuade people to pledge their loyalty and worship to the first Beast, and people are led to worship his "image," and if anyone refuses, the second beast will have them killed (13:13–15). Curiously, John says that the image of the Beast is empowered, in some way, to "even speak" as if it were alive (13:15). Revelation 13 ends with an account of how this second beast introduces a mark of identification on all those who would receive it—the famous "mark of the beast" (13:16–18).

Later, in chapter 17, the Beast is mentioned again with further clues that help us identify him. We encounter a woman described as "a great prostitute," with whom "the kings of the earth have committed sexual immorality" (17:1–2). She is first described as "seated on many waters" (17:1), but then the vision shifts to a wilderness, where John sees the woman "sitting on a scarlet beast that was full of blasphemous names, and it had seven heads and ten horns" (17:3). This is the first Beast from the sea John described in chapter 13. The woman is dressed in the apparel of luxury and wealth. Along with being "arrayed in purple and scarlet, and adorned with gold, jewels and pearls," she also possesses a "golden cup" that is full of sin and evil—"full of abominations and the impurities of her sexual immorality" (17:4).

John goes on to add that her name is inked on her forehead. It's a "name of mystery: Babylon the great, mother of prostitutes and of earth's abominations" (17:5). When John says her name, "Babylon the great," is a "mystery," he poses a riddle to his readers. But it's not a riddle he wishes to keep under lock and key. He is inviting them to solve it. As it turns out, the word "Babylon" was a Jewish and Christian nickname for a well-known entity of the first century. Its meaning was easily discernible. More on that in a moment.

The angel guiding John in the vision notices his bewilderment and asks, "'Why do you marvel? I will tell you the mystery of the woman, and of the beast with seven heads and ten horns that carries her'" (17:7). The angel then interprets the vision, saying, "The beast you saw was, and is not, and is about to rise from the bottomless pit and go to destruction" (17:8a). This illustrates how the Beast is a counterfeit of God, who was earlier described as one "who is and who was and who is to come, the Almighty" (Rev 1:8). The angel, apparently, sees the Beast as a pitiful parody of the one true God.[2]

When the angel describes the seven heads and ten horns of the Beast, he says his explanation "calls for a mind with wisdom" (17:9). The point here is that the Beast is a symbol, a picture, of some other reality. It takes wisdom, he says. This symbolic Beast is not, in other words, something so secretive that it cannot be unlocked. The mystery is discernible.

The angel goes on to say the seven heads of the Beast represent "seven mountains on which the woman is seated" (17:9). They also represent "seven kings" (17:10). The angel elaborates further about these seven kings, saying that five of these seven kings "have fallen"

---

2. "The threefold description of God found already in 1:8; 4:8; 11:16; and 16:5 is reapplied to the beast—to mock the beast. The interjection of the negative—'is not'—and 'coming up' parodies Christ's death and resurrection (compare the threefold formula of Jesus's death and resurrection in 1:18a; 2:8). That the beast 'is not' refers to the continuing effects of his defeat by Christ at the cross and resurrection (see on 13:3, where 'death' is the equivalent negative expression to 'is not')." G. K. Beale, *The Book of Revelation: A Commentary on the Greek Text*, NIGTC (Grand Rapids: Eerdmans, 1999), 864.

(that is, *died*), the sixth king currently "is" (that is, still *alive*), and the seventh king "has not yet come," but "when he does come he must remain only a little while" (17:10). So while the image of the Beast that John sees is one entity, it is at the same time a conglomerate of *multiple* entities—of seven kings, that is.

This is how the angel can go on to say that one Beast is also at the same time a symbol for an "eighth" head. After describing the seven heads of the Beast, the angel says of the Beast itself: "As for the beast that was and is not, it is an eighth but it belongs to the seven, and it goes to destruction" (17:11). Apparently, the Beast itself is connected in some way to the seven kings (he "belongs to the seven").

Next, the angel describes the ten horns. They each represent ten different kings, he says, who are in positions of authority along with the Beast (17:12). They actually "hand over their power and authority to the beast" and "make war on the Lamb," though "the Lamb will conquer them" (17:13–14). The point is that Jesus is the true "Lord of lords and King of kings" (17:14). The emphasis again seems to be political. Who is in charge? Is it the Beast? The kings in league with the Beast? The truth—the big *reveal*—is that the Lamb is in charge. In God's economy, the slain Lamb is more powerful than any monstrous Beast, no matter how ferocious it is. Again, the point of this story is not to spread fear among Christians. To the contrary, the goal is to identify the early Christians' fear and then remind them that they actually have nothing to fear because Jesus, the Lamb, is stronger than the Beast.

But what, exactly, do the Beast and the prostitute represent? What do these characters symbolize? We get closer to an answer when we notice how the angel explains the other parts of John's vision. The prostitute represents "the great city that has dominion over the kings of the earth" (17:18). In Revelation 18, the prostitute/great city is once again called "Babylon," with whom "the kings of the earth have committed immorality" and with whom "the merchants of the earth have grown rich from the power of her luxurious living" (18:2–3).

UNDERSTANDING THE SYMBOLS

The descriptions of the two beasts, the prostitute, and the various kings of the earth can appear confusing and convoluted—especially on a first reading. It's a rather odd vision, to say the least. Yet, John does not expect his readers to be confused. With a bit of wisdom, the symbols and images *can* be interpreted. Admittedly, for those of us living some two thousand years later, the text can be quite challenging. Not so for those living in first-century Asia. These images would have been very familiar to his original audience.[3]

If we adopt the reading strategy discussed in the previous chapter, we can interpret John's visions fairly easily, too. Remember, this letter to the seven churches must have been understandable and discernible (Rev 13:18; 17:9). These seven churches needed encouragement. They were living in a world filled with Roman propaganda about the emperor and his supposed worthiness to be worshiped and adored.

What does this have to do with Revelation's Beast? *Everything.* The Beast seems to be a symbol for the Roman Empire. It's John's way of unveiling Rome's monstrosity and exposing the empire's depravity. Notice, for example, how John describes the seven heads of the Beast as "seven mountains" (17:9). In the first century, the city of Rome was commonly associated with the seven hills it was built on.[4] In one ancient text known as the Sibylline Oracles, the city is referred to as the "seven-hilled Rome" (2.18).[5] G. B. Caird says that even before the time John wrote to the seven churches, "Rome had been known as *urbs septicollis,*" that is, *the city of seven hills.* He adds that "the festival of Septimontium was celebrated every year in December to commemorate the enclosure of the seven hills within

---

3. See deSilva, *Discovering Revelation,* 147–48.

4. For a list of ancient references, see G. B. Caird, *The Revelation of St. John the Divine* (New York: Harper & Row, 1966), 216; see also deSilva, *Discovering Revelation,* 148. For a history of Rome's association with seven hills, see David E. Aune, *Revelation 17–22,* WBC (Dallas: Thomas Nelson, 1998), 944–45.

5. This translation comes from J. J. Collins, "Sibylline Oracles," *OTP* 1:317–472. Regardless of the date of this text (see Collins, "Sibylline Oracles," 1:331–32), the association of Rome with the seven hills began before the writing of Revelation.

her walls (Suet. *Dom* 4)."[6] In his biography of the emperor Domitian, the ancient historian Suetonius mentions a scene where Domitian "gave a splendid banquet" in order "to celebrate the Feast of the Seven Hills." He describes a feast in which a huge amount of food was consumed and gifts were bestowed by the emperor (*Dom.* 4). Most anyone living in the Roman Empire would have been familiar with such festivities, and they certainly would have understood John's "seven mountains" (*hepta orē*) reference as pointing to Rome.[7]

A modern equivalent is how most Americans (and many people around the world) refer to New York City as "the Big Apple." Most people today are familiar with this nickname, but people living two thousand years from now would have a hard time deciphering the meaning of it—unless, of course, they had access to historical sources from our own era that could guide them. Just as "the Big Apple" refers to New York City, so *the city on seven hills* refers to Rome.

It makes sense, then, why John will go on to say that the seven hills also represent seven kings (17:10). The city of Rome was the capital of the empire, where her rulers lived and reigned. On the one hand, the Beast symbolizes a singular entity (Rev 13). At the same time, it also represents multiple entities—various kings/heads (17:9). But how can it represent both? The vision might be difficult to imagine for us, but we can't forget this is *apocalyptic* literature. Revelation communicates truth through the power of mythic symbolism, which is able to possess many layers of meaning at once.

The same goes for all the associated images connected to the Beast as well—including the woman riding the Beast. Recall how the woman was described as "the great city" and as "Babylon" (Rev 17:18; 18:2–3). This means the entire image of the Beast—from the woman to the Beast itself to the seven heads—is intended to evoke an

---

6. Caird, *Revelation*, 216.

7. Note how the ESV translates *hepta orē* as "seven mountains," while the NIV has "seven hills." On "hills" and "mountains," Aune helpfully observes that "Roman writers often used the terms *mons*, 'mountain,' and *collis*, 'hill,' interchangeably when referring to the Seven Hills of Rome" (*Revelation 17–22*, 945; see sources cited there).

apocalyptic image of the imperial city and, by extension, the Roman Empire. It's an apocalyptic image because it *reveals* the truth about the Roman Empire: it is immoral, corrupt, and inspired by Satan. The prostitute, for example, represents the city of Rome's economic prowess and exploitation of other nations. Rome was well-known for gaining wealth and power by immoral deeds such as exploiting other nations for her economic benefit.[8] Her wealth is depicted as luxurious clothing, and she holds a golden cup that is full of evil (17:4). This signifies her corrupt "dominion over the kings of the earth" (17:18). In Revelation 18, her wealth is interpreted as part of the reason for her demise:

> her sins are heaped high as heaven,
>   and God has remembered her iniquities.
> Pay her back as she herself has paid back others,
>   and repay her double for her deeds;
>   mix a double portion for her in the cup she mixed.
> As she glorified herself and lived in luxury,
>   so give her a like measure of torment and mourning,
> since in her heart she says,
>
> "I sit as a queen,
> I am no widow,
>   and mourning I shall never see." (18:5–7)

> Alas, alas, for the great city
> that was clothed in fine linen,
>   in purple and scarlet,
> adorned with gold,
>   with jewels, and with pearls! (18:16)

---

8. See the helpful discussions in deSilva, *Discovering Revelation*, 50–54, 150–51, 154–63. He notes specifically that "a major focus of John's indictment of 'Babylon' is the exploitive nature of its global economy, structured to secure the near-endless consumption of resources from every province and beyond by the population at the centre and, of course, the local provincial elites who support the system" (155).

So will Babylon the great city be thrown down with violence,
and will be found no more ...
for your merchants were the great ones of the earth,
and all nations were deceived by your sorcery.
And in her was found the blood of prophets and of saints,
and all who have been slain on earth. (18:21, 23–24)

John also calls the woman "Babylon" to draw attention to the similarities between the two empires. "Babylon" was a nickname for Rome among Jews and Christians. One important similarity was how Rome destroyed Jerusalem and the temple, just like Babylonian Empire had done previously.[9]

To sum up, here is what we have observed about the identity of the Beast:

1. John connects the Beast with "a great city" (17:18; 18:10, 16–19);

2. John connects the Beast with seven mountains/hills, which also at the same time symbolize seven political figures (17:9–10);

3. John describes the Beast as an entity having political and military authority (13:2, 7; 17:10) that also receives worship (13:4, 8, 12–15);

4. John links the Beast with the term "Babylon," which was a well-known synonym in the first century for Rome (18:1, 10).

Given that John intends for his letter to be discernible to his original readers (1:3) and that his original readers also lived in the Roman

9. DeSilva, *Discovering Revelation*, 147–48.

Empire (1:11), the conclusions drawn above seem to fit. The evidence points directly to the Roman Empire.

NOT ONE MARK BUT TWO

Knowing John equates the Beast with the Roman Empire, let's revisit the overall question for this chapter: What is the mark of the Beast? Here's the relevant passage:

> Also [the second Beast] causes all, both small and great, both rich and poor, both free and slave, to be marked on the right hand or the forehead, so that no one can buy or sell unless he has the mark, that is, the name of the beast or the number of its name. This calls for wisdom: let the one who has understanding calculate the number of the beast, for it is the number of a man, and his number is 666. (Rev 13:16–18)

Here John says the second Beast enforces a "mark" of loyalty on people—a mark that goes either on their "right hand or the forehead" (13:16). The mark itself is associated with the Beast's name or, mysteriously, with "the number of its name" (13:17). That number is the well-known "666."

Before we get too deep into this passage, it's important to realize that the mark of the Beast is not the only mark Revelation talks about. John *also* mentions a mark for the righteous. In fact, it's in the very next verse: "Then I looked, and behold, on Mount Zion stood the Lamb, and with him 144,000 who had his name and his Father's name written on their foreheads" (Rev 14:1).

The parallels between the two passages are interesting. The wicked receive a mark on their forehead (or right hand), and the righteous receive a mark on their forehead. Additionally, both marks are associated with names: the mark on the wicked is a man's name, and the mark on the righteous is the Lamb's and the Father's name. In Revelation 7, John already reported seeing the righteous receiving a mark on their foreheads. He describes it as a "seal." Notice what he says:

> After this I saw four angels standing at the four corners of the earth, holding back the four winds of the earth, that no wind might blow on earth or sea or against any tree. Then I saw another angel ascending from the rising of the sun, with the seal of the living God, and he called with a loud voice to the four angels who had been given power to harm earth and sea, saying, "Do not harm the earth or the sea or the trees, until we have sealed the servants of our God on their foreheads." (Rev 7:1–3)

One scholar describes this mark on God's people as "the mark of the Lamb."[10] When we take Revelation 7 and 14 together, we can better discern what this mark is all about. It has two functions: to *identify* and *protect*. Notice how the earth was not to be struck with God's wrath until "the servants of our God" received a seal "on their foreheads" (7:3). This seal—or mark—identifies the people of God in order to protect them from the wrath to come.

None of this is original to Revelation. There are precursors in early Jewish literature that also speak about marks on the righteous and unrighteous. In Ezekiel, for example, God directs an angel to "put a mark on the foreheads" of the righteous so that they will be spared from the coming destruction (Ezek 9:4). This mark is to signal to other angels to leave them alone—in other words, not to strike them. They are to "touch no one on whom is the mark" (9:6).[11] In the Psalms of Solomon, an early Jewish text written several decades before Christ's birth, there is a discussion about how "the sign of God is upon the righteous ones for salvation" (15.8).[12] Regarding the wicked, this text also says, "the sign of destruction is upon their forehead" (15.10).

---

10. Craig Keener, "What Is the Mark of the Beast? Craig S. Keener Explains," YouTube, January 10, 2018, https://www.youtube.com/watch?v=r3eIWA9XS04.

11. Keener thinks John's reference to the "seal" in Rev 7:3–4 "alludes" to the passage in Ezek 9:4–6 (*Revelation*, 353).

12. On the date of Psalms of Solomon, see R. B. Wright, "Psalms of Solomon: A New Translation and Introduction," OTP 2:640–41.

New Testament scholar Craig Keener makes an important observation about all this: "Both Ezekiel's mark on the righteous and the mark on the wicked in the Psalms of Solomon are symbolic marks visible only to God and his angels, not to people."[13] In other words, these are marks of spiritual identity. They do not make a person righteous or unrighteous as much as they identify them as such. It's reasonable to think, therefore, that Revelation's mark of the Beast and mark of the Lamb operate in the same way: they identify the righteous and the wicked, and they are signs of protection and destruction. When John speaks about the "seal," he is similar to Paul, who describes Christians as being "sealed with the promised Holy Spirit" (Eph 1:13).

All of this is helpful background information for interpreting both the mark of the Beast and the mark of the Lamb. At the end of the day, they are simply marks of identification that reveal where a person's loyalty resides. And like the passages from Ezekiel, Psalms of Solomon, and Ephesians, it is most likely the case that neither of these marks in Revelation is visible.

THE MARK IS ALL ABOUT WORSHIP

In Revelation 13, the second beast convinces people to *both* make an image of the first Beast for the purpose of worship *and* take the Beast's mark (13:14–17). This suggests that worshiping the Beast and taking his mark are two sides of the same coin. Other passages in Revelation say something similar:

> They have no rest, day or night, these worshipers of the beast and its image, and whoever receives the mark of its name. (Rev 14:11)

> So the first angel went and poured out his bowl on the earth, and harmful and painful sores came upon the people who bore the mark of the beast and worshiped its image. (Rev 16:2)

> And the beast was captured, and with it the false prophet who in its presence had done the signs by which he deceived those

---

13. Keener, *Revelation*, 353.

who had received the mark of the beast and those who worshiped its image. (Rev 19:20)

Whatever the mark of the Beast is, it seems to be connected with overt worship of the Beast. There is no hint that the mark is something people can accidentally accept. Revelation doesn't teach a person can take the mark without knowing what they are doing. To the contrary, accepting the mark of the Beast is tantamount to worshiping the Beast—which is something you do on purpose. Again, the mark of the Beast is a mark of identification: it *marks out* those who worship the Beast. Similarly, the mark of the Lamb *marks out* those who reject the ways of the world and accept Christ. The wicked are marked for destruction, and the righteous are marked for protection from destruction. At the end of the day, both marks are all about worship.

What shape does this worship take? In the above passages, the Beast is worshiped through an image. The second Beast instructs people "to make an image for the beast that was wounded by the sword and yet lived. And it was allowed to give breath to the image of the beast, so that the image of the beast might even speak and might cause those who would not worship the image of the beast to be slain" (Rev 13:14–15; see also Rev 16:2; 19:20).

In John's day, images were routinely used for worship. As we saw in the last chapter, the seven cities to which Revelation was written were thick with all sorts of pagan temples. There was no lack of images of gods and goddesses in these cities. Images of Caesar were everywhere, too. So when John talks about the Beast's image, his readers would have associated it with the Roman emperor.

IMAGES OF WORSHIP:
COINS AND STATUES

In the Roman-occupied world, it would not have been unusual to find an imperial coin with the image of the emperor on it. This is nothing unique to the first century. Many countries, including my own (the United States), stamp images of (past) political leaders on their coins.

Such images serve to remind citizens of their shared political history, values, and the like. Ancient Rome was no exception, but it went further. It struck images of emperors on coins that Jews and Christians found overtly blasphemous. These coins often bore "allusions to the emperor's divinity."[14]

This was certainly true in Jesus's day. It would have been easy to find a Roman coin with the image of the emperor Tiberius stamped on it along with the phrase "son of the divine Augustus." This was a reference to his father and the previous emperor, Caesar Augustus, who had been deified several years before.[15] Such blasphemies could also be found on coins later during the reign of Nero. The same goes with Domitian, who was emperor when Revelation was written to the seven churches.[16] It's safe to say that the original readers of Revelation would have easily connected the dots between *Beast* and *image* and *worship* and *imperial coinage*. Coins were literally *marked* with the Beast's image and with his claims to be divine.

Caesar's image was not associated with just coins, but also with statues that were worshiped.[17] Recall how John associates the Beast's

---

14. Keener, *Revelation*, 352.

15. Kraybill, *Apocalypse and Allegiance*, 150n18, 151. Kraybill goes on to discuss the well-known exchange between Jesus and a Pharisee about whether it was okay to pay taxes to Caesar (Matt 22:15–22). He says, "As a radical Jew, Jesus carries no Roman money on his person. But when he asks for a coin, one of his critics compromises himself by producing a *denarius*. Jesus asks whose image (*eikōn*) and whose title is on it, thus forcing his Jewish opponents to admit that they are carrying money inscribed with blasphemous claims. Then Jesus answers the question about paying taxes: 'Give therefore to the emperor the things that are the emperor's, and to God the things that are God's' (Matt. 22:21). In other words, let the idolatrous emperor have the coins bearing his icon. Human beings, made in the image (*eikōn*) of their Creator, belong wholly to God" (*Apocalypse and Allegiance*, 150, emphasis original). See also David L. Vagi, *Coinage and History of the Roman Empire* (Chicago: Fitzroy Dearborn, 1999), 2:241–45.

16. "Many first-century Roman coins bore legends such as 'Emperor Caesar Domitian Augustus, Son of the Divine Vespasian, Pontifex Maximus [Chief Priest].' Coins of Nero and Domitian sometimes portrayed those emperors with the spiked crown associated with divinity. Jewish rebels, known as Zealots for their claim of radical obedience to God, refused to carry or even look at such money" (Kraybill, *Apocalypse and Allegiance*, 149–50).

17. Perhaps modern nations are not as far from this in the way we treat our leaders as we might like to think. On a recent trip to Washington, DC, my family and I visited the Lincoln Memorial. The memorial is made to resemble an ancient Greek temple, and an impressive statue of Abraham Lincoln is the main attraction. The statue depicts Lincoln as a leader sitting

image with worship. His readers knew Caesar was worshiped by nearly everyone in Asia. But is there any historical evidence that speaks of Caesar's image being worshiped? As it turns out, the answer is yes.

In AD 112, not long after John wrote Revelation, the governor of Bithynia (a province right next to Asia, where John's seven churches were) wrote to the emperor Trajan to get legal advice about how to handle Christians in the area.[18] This governor, named Pliny, tells the emperor that his standard practice has been to interrogate those who are accused of being Christians. Anyone who fails to recant their Christian faith will be executed—mainly, says Pliny, because of their "obstinacy" (*Letters* 10.96).[19] Pliny goes on to describe the test he gives to the accused—an examination that includes paying homage to Trajan's statue. Here's what he says:

> An anonymous pamphlet has been circulated which contains the names of a number of accused persons. Among these I considered that I should dismiss any who denied that they were or ever had been Christians when they had repeated after me a formula of invocation to the gods and had made offerings of wine and incense to your statue (which I had ordered to be brought into court for this purpose along with the images of the gods), and furthermore had reviled the name of Christ: none of which things, I understand, any genuine Christian can be induced to do. Others, whose names were given to me by an informer, first admitted the charge and then denied it; they said that they had ceased to be Christians two or more years previously, and some

---

on a throne of sorts. The political aspect of the image is evident, but so is the religious. Behind Lincoln there is etched into the wall the following statement: "In this temple / as in the hearts of the people / for whom he saved the union / the memory of Abraham Lincoln / is enshrined forever."

18. Everett Ferguson, *Church History*, vol. 1, *From Christ to Pre-Reformation: The Rise and Growth of the Church in Its Cultural, Intellectual, and Political Context* (Grand Rapids: Zondervan, 2005), 69.

19. All quotations from Pliny are taken from Pliny, *Letters and Panegyiricus*, ed. G. P. Goold, trans. Betty Radice, 2 vols. (Cambridge: Harvard University Press, 1975).

of them even twenty years ago. They all did reverence to your
statue and the images of the gods in the same way as the others,
and reviled the name of Christ. (Pliny, *Letters* 10.96)

This passage comes from within two decades of the writing of Revelation
and was written from a nearby province, and there is no suggestion that
the worship of Caesar's image was Pliny's invention. It is not a stretch
of the imagination to assume similar practices were happening in Asia
as well. In fact, as we have seen, Asia was a prime place where such
things did happen. Pliny's letter provides evidence that Caesar's image
was worshiped, *and* it demonstrates what the consequences were if
Christians refused: death. This is the exact situation John describes
when he talks about worshiping the image of the Beast, which is associated with the mark. The mark of the Beast, though, is associated with
a name—that is, with a certain emperor. But which one?

NERO AND 666

As I mentioned above, Revelation was most likely written during the
reign of Domitian. He, along with the emperors Caligula and Nero
before him, insisted on being worshiped while he was alive. Describing
Domitian's hubris, the ancient writer Suetonius says, "'Lord and God'
became his regular title both in writing and conversation" (*Dom.* 13).
Domitian was quite the megalomaniac—and a powerful one at that.

Several years before Domitian, Nero also embarked on his own
reign of terror. He famously blamed the great fire of Rome on Christians,
persecuting them in the most heinous of ways as a result (Tacitus,
Annals 15.44). A savage ruler to the core, he was well-known for having
murdered his own mother (*Annals* 14.3–9; Suetonius, *Nero* 34). Because
of Nero's perverse scruples and blasphemous claims to deity, many
scholars think John's reference to the Beast has something to do with
Nero.[20] Here's how what John says about the Beast points to Nero.

---

20. Gorman is correct to observe that "perhaps the majority of scholars today" see Nero
as the referent for Revelation's 666 (*Reading Revelation*, 127).

The Beast's number, 666, may signal a "parody of perfection," since each digit is one less than 777—a number often taken to symbolize perfection.[21] In the ancient world, it was common to give numerical values to words, phrases, and names of people—a practice called *gematria*.[22] Each letter of the alphabet had a number associated with it. Languages such as Greek and Hebrew did not have separate scripts for writing numbers. Those who wrote in these languages would have to use their respective alphabets to serve also as numbers.[23] Using gematria, when you take Nero's name in Greek (*nerōn kaisar*) and transliterate it into Hebrew equivalents (*nrwn qsr*), you get 666. Interestingly, if you use an alternate spelling for Nero's name, dropping the final *n* (*nerō kaisar*), you get the number 616. This may be significant because in some manuscripts of Revelation, the number given for the name of the Beast is not 666 but 616.[24] As one scholar says, "This change suggests that the scribes knew the tradition of the name that the number should spell, and respelled it accordingly!"[25]

When it comes to Nero and gematria, Suetonius records how citizens of Rome publicly mocked and ridiculed Nero by spreading riddles and jokes about him throughout the city—in both written and oral form. One instance of mockery included a gematria-laced riddle about Nero killing his own mother. Suetonius says the riddle went like this:

---

21. Gorman, *Reading Revelation*, 126.

22. On gematria, as well as a few examples of it from the ancient world, see Kraybill, *Apocalypse and Allegiance*, 65–67.

23. This is much different from, say, my own American culture. The English alphabet is not used also for numbers because Americans have adopted a separate script for numbering—namely, the Arabic system.

24. On all of this (gematria, Nero, 666, and 616), see Gorman, *Reading Revelation*, 126–27. See also Wilson, "Early Christians," 184n22; Kraybill, *Apocalypse and Allegiance*, 65–67. Gorman also mentions how the numbers 666 and 616 can be reached when playing with well-known abbreviations of Domitian's titles and Caligula's name, respectively (*Reading Revelation*, 128).

25. Keener, *Revelation*, 356.

> Count the numerical values
>   Of the letters in Nero's name,
> And in "murdered his own mother":
>   You will find their sum is the same. (Suetonius, *Nero* 39)

In other words, if you add up each letter of Nero's name, it will equal the sum of the entire phrase "murdered his own mother."[26]

Here's why this is important. In the first century, Nero's name was routinely being trifled with—and criticized.[27] John, too, criticizes Rome by calling her "Babylon." To say that John is also critiquing the despotic emperor by using a riddle of gematria wouldn't be a stretch. Like Nero's other critics in the first century, John might very well be doing something similar with 666.

But there's more historical evidence that ties the Beast to Nero. In some ancient texts, Nero is either compared to a Beast or flat-out called one. One scholar says,

> Nero is twice compared to a beast … by Apollonius (Philostratus *Vit. Apoll.* 4:38). Indeed, he is much worse because no animal "devours its own mother, but Nero is gorged with such quarry." Nero is also called a great beast … in the Sybilline Oracles (8.157). Domitian is similarly called "the most monstrous beast" by Pliny the Younger (*immanissima belua*; *Pan.* 48:3), but this in the context of describing him as a *Nero redivivus*. Juvenal (*Sat* 4.38) likewise thought of Domitian as a second, albeit bald, Nero, and Martial (*Epig.* 11:33) referred to Domitian's death as Nero's.[28]

---

26. Here the number is not 666 but rather 1,005 (Grant's edition of Suetonius' *The Twelve Caesars*, 347n18). This doesn't mean Nero isn't Revelation's "666." Names could have many different numbers associated with them, depending on how one chose to spell the name and which names were used.

27. "Among the Roman emperors Suetonius mentions only Nero as having gematria associated with his name (*Ner.* 39.2)" (Wilson, "Early Christians," 184).

28. Wilson, "Early Christians," 185. On Sibylline Oracles 8, see also deSilva, *Discovering Revelation*, 149; compare Keener, *Revelation*, 338. On Pliny's comparison of Domitian to Nero, see also *Pan.* 53.4 (Bandy, *Revelation*, 74n101). It should be pointed out that some texts mentioned here are dated rather late. For example, Sibylline Oracles 8.157 has been dated roughly

All of this is helpful evidence in helping us figure out what Revelation's Beast refers to. In this quote, you probably noticed the phrase "Nero redivivus." This refers to an early legend or myth that sprung up sometime after Nero's death. The legend was that one day Nero would return to lead an army and destroy his enemies, along with anyone else who stood in his way. The idea was that Nero would return because he never actually died (Nero *redux*) or because he would rise from the dead (Nero *redivivus*).[29] In John's vision, the Beast is depicted as being resurrected, perhaps because "the beast represents a parody of Christ who died and rose again and who will come again to conquer the world kingdoms."[30] Most likely, John does not intend for us to interpret the Beast's resurrection *literally* but rather *literarily*. It is presented as a symbolic counterfeit of Christ's actual resurrection.

Several ancient sources report that pretenders rose up claiming to be Nero around the time Revelation was written.[31] Suetonius reports, for instance, that twenty years after Nero's death, about AD 88, "a mysterious individual came forward claiming to be Nero" (*Nero* 57). He goes on to say that this pretender gathered support from the Parthians. The Parthian Empire sat east of the Roman Empire and was considered one of Rome's dreaded enemies. The claim that Nero had returned with Parthian support would have sent chills down the spines of the Roman elite. The rumor of Nero's return would also have

---

to AD 175, some eighty years after Revelation was written. See Hans-Josef Klauck, "Do They Never Come Back? *Nero Redivivus* and the Apocalypse of John," *CBQ* 63 (October 2001): 688. That said, such texts remain valuable as they represent ancient perspectives about Nero and Domitian—perspectives that were most likely inherited from an even earlier era, perhaps even John's.

29. "A myth emerged that Nero had not actually died or that he would come back to life and retake the imperial throne. Ancient pagan and Christian sources mention what came to be called the Nero redivivus (Nero resurrected) legend" (Kraybill, *Apocalypse and Allegiance*, 65). Compare Klauck, "Do They Never Come Back?"; David E. Aune, *Revelation 6–16*, WBC (Dallas: Thomas Nelson, 1998), 737–40, esp. 738 on the distinction between "Nero *redux*" and "Nero *redivivus*." See also Bandy, *Revelation*, 71–74, esp. 74.

30. Bandy, *Revelation*, 74. See again Rev 13:4, 12, 14; 17:10–12.

31. See deSilva, *Discovering Revelation*, 149 (and sources cited there).

been well-known to John, especially given that the incident reported by Suetonius occurred just a few years before he penned Revelation.[32]

Because of the parallels between Nero and Domitian, it is also possible that John thinks Domitian is the Nero *redivivus*. But as many scholars point out, John means this figuratively—Domitian is the new Nero the way John the Baptist is the new Elijah (Matt 11:11–15).

THE BEAST: MORE THAN
AN INDIVIDUAL

In spite of the background that leads us to associate the Beast with particular emperors, though, I don't think the Beast can be reduced to just Nero or Domitian.[33] In Revelation 13:3, John says the seven-headed Beast had one head that "seemed to have a mortal wound, but its mortal wound was healed, and the whole earth marveled as they followed the beast." Even though John can speak of one of the heads of the Beast as wounded but "healed" (13:3), he transfers this language to the Beast as a whole, saying it was "wounded by the sword and yet lived" (13:14; see also 13:12).[34] This implies that this wounded-but-healed head of the Beast is not merely a part of the Beast but is connected to the essence of the Beast itself. For John, what is true of the wounded head is at the same time true of the Beast as a whole.

Because Nero died by suicide—a knife to the throat, in fact—and each of the seven heads represents a Roman emperor, John's "mortal wound" passage does most likely refer to Nero's death, and the Beast's healed wound most likely refers to the Nero *redivivus* myth. And as I said above, for John the new Nero might be Domitian. But the Beast

---

32. Keener is right to caution, however, that "The date depends on Suetonius's estimate" (*Revelation*, 338n12; on the Parthians, see 270–71).

33. So Gorman, *Reading Revelation*, 124–25, 128. Kraybill says: "Although it seems likely that John meant 666 to refer to Nero, we should not limit the meaning of the number of the beast or the symbol of the beast to one demented ruler. Structural evil in Revelation is bigger than the reign of Nero; any human entity that usurps allegiance that belongs to God is beastly. It is possible the number six, used three times, simply was an abstract symbol for John" (*Apocalypse and Allegiance*, 67).

34. Aune, *Revelation 6–16*, 736. He says, "While in v 3a it is one of the seven heads of the first beast that is wounded, in vv 12 and 14 it is the beast itself that is mortally wounded" (736).

means something more than Nero or Domitian. As David deSilva writes, "Nero is not merely one aberrant head among others: he gives the beast its character."[35]

We also see this idea in Revelation 17:9–11, where John gives us more information regarding the seven-headed Beast. The seven heads, as mentioned above, represent the seven mountains of Rome (17:9). The seven heads also represent "seven kings"—a reference to Rome's political leaders, the emperors (17:10a). John elaborates further about the Beast and its seven heads, saying, "They are also seven kings, five of whom have fallen, one is, the other has not yet come, and when he does come he must remain only a little while. As for the beast that was and is not, it is an eighth but it belongs to the seven, and it goes to destruction" (17:10–11).

John is saying that five of the emperors have already died, one of them is still alive, and one of them hasn't arrived yet (at the time of John's writing). This makes seven kings total. But John also describes the Beast as "an eighth" king that belongs, mysteriously, to the previous seven (17:11). This, too, most likely refers to the myth of Nero's return.[36] As I said above, this may very well be Domitian or some other Nero-like emperor after him.[37] Either way, it doesn't seem to refer to *just* one individual as a second Nero. The eighth king, after all, embodies and symbolizes all that the Beast is. This is similar to how John spoke of the Beast's mortal wound as being a wound on the individual head of the Beast *and* of the entire Beast itself (see again Rev 13:3, 12, 14).

WHO ARE THESE EIGHT KINGS?

Scholars have long debated the identity of these eight kings, with no agreement being reached.[38] Visualizing a list of emperors from John's era might be helpful. According to Suetonius, who wrote the

---

35. DeSilva, *Unholy Allegiances*, 46.

36. See again deSilva, *Unholy Allegiances*, 46; see also Kraybill, *Apocalypse and Allegiance*, 130.

37. See the discussion in Kraybill, *Apocalypse and Allegiance*, 126–27.

38. For a summary of the various perspectives, see Osborne, *Revelation* [2002], 617–21.

well-known ancient biographies of Rome's first imperial leaders (called *The Twelve Caesars*), the list includes the following:

1. Julius Caesar

2. Augustus

3. Tiberius

4. Gaius (Caligula)

5. Claudius

6. Nero

7. Galba

8. Otho

9. Vitellius

10. Vespasian

11. Titus

12. Domitian

John says that "five have fallen" and "one is" (Rev 17:10). If we start with Julius Caesar, then the first five who have fallen would be Julius Caesar through Claudius. This would mean that Nero is the emperor who "is"—that is, still alive when John wrote Revelation. It is certainly possible that Nero was the reigning emperor when John penned his letter. However, the arguments for a date during Domitian's reign in the 90s are, in my opinion, far more persuasive.[39] As deSilva argues, one clue that suggests John wrote during Domitian's reign is that the healing of the Beast's (= Rome's) "mortal wound" (Rev 13:3) probably doesn't make sense until after both the death of Nero and the subsequent

---

39. See again Osborne, *Revelation* [2002], 6–9, esp. 9; see also deSilva, *Discovering Revelation*, 35–39.

civil war. It was not until Vespasian that the empire was stabilized again. According to deSilva, worship of the emperor "experienced something of a revival during the Flavian dynasty, particularly under Domitian."[40] We might also consider how Revelation refers to Rome as "Babylon." Rome receives this epithet because of her many similarities with ancient Babylon. Like Babylon, Rome sacked Jerusalem and destroyed the Jewish temple in AD 70, which was *after* Nero's suicide. This, too, suggests Revelation was written after, and not during, Nero's reign. Besides, it is not altogether clear that we should start the list with Julius Caesar anyway. The ancient sources appear divided as to who— either Julius or Augustus—should be counted as the first emperor.

If we start with Augustus as the beginning of the five kings who have fallen, then the fifth would be Nero. This means that Galba would be the sixth king, who was still alive, with Otho being the seventh. This makes Vitellius the eighth emperor. The problem with this scenario, however, is that all three of these emperors (Galba, Otho, and Vitellius) were insignificant in the grand scheme of things. Added together, their time as emperors lasted only about a year. None of them belonged to the original Julian dynasty, and they only came to power after Nero killed himself. After Nero's death, the empire was plunged into civil war, resulting in power-hungry individuals vying for the throne. According to Suetonius, the empire suffered greatly under these three emperors, leaving it in a state of instability. The empire wasn't stabilized, he says, until the reign of the Flavian dynasty (Vespasian and his sons Titus and Domitian).[41] For this reason, some scholars exclude Galba, Otho, and Vitellius from the list of John's eight kings altogether.[42]

That being so, if we begin with Augustus and skip these three interim leaders, this leaves Vespasian as John's sixth "king" (and

---

40. DeSilva, *Discovering Revelation*, 37. See also 38.

41. Says Suetonius: "The family of the Flavians at last brought stable government to the Empire; they had found it drifting uneasily through the usurpations and deaths of three successive emperors" (*Vespasian* 1).

42. See, e.g., Klauck, "Do They Never Come Back," 696–97.

hence the current emperor), with his sons Titus and Domitian as the seventh and eighth, respectively. The advantage of this theory is that it makes sense of Revelation 17:10, which says the seventh king will "remain only a little while." Titus only reigned for a short period, so his role as the seventh under this arrangement seems to fit.[43] One potential problem with this is that the three emperors after Nero—even though it's true they never stabilized the empire—were still considered emperors by some in the ancient world. Suetonius, for example, depicts them as emperors.[44] So, this view leaves us with some uncertainty. Of course, there are other options. One might begin the list with other emperors and calculate from there.[45] But I'm not convinced any of these ways are as fruitful as we would like them to be. It seems to me that we need another way to look at John's list of eight kings.

Most likely, John doesn't intend for his readers to worry about finding the identity of each of the Beast's heads. Even though the seven heads certainly refer to seven historical emperors of the first century, taken together they most likely have symbolic meaning. Here's how this works. Some scholars think John's vision of a seven-headed monster is a merging of four beasts that Daniel saw in the vision recorded in Daniel 7.[46] There's a lot of similarity between Daniel's vision and John's, and John was obviously familiar with Daniel's vision of four "beasts" that arise from the sea (Dan 7:3). In Daniel's vision, the first beast is described "like a lion" (7:4), the second beast "like a bear" (7:5), and the third beast is "like a leopard" that has "four heads" (7:6). The fourth beast has "ten horns," along with another "little horn" that comes up among the other horns (7:7–8). Each of the four beasts are interpreted as "four kings" that

---

43. On this, see Klauck, "Do They Never Come Back," 696–97.

44. Although, because Suetonius also describes their reigns as "usurpations" (*Vespasian* 1), some question the legitimacy and significance of their reigns, thus excluding them from the list of kings (Aune, *Revelation 17–22*, 947).

45. On this, see the various options presented in Aune, *Revelation 17–22*, 947.

46. Witherington, *Revelation*, 180–81; deSilva, *Discovering Revelation*, 36–37.

represent four kingdoms (7:17).[47] Daniel is later told the ten horns of the fourth beast symbolize kings (7:24).

Now recall John's description of the Beast: it resembles a leopard with bear's feet and a lion's mouth, rises from the sea, and has ten horns and seven heads (Rev 13:1–2). It is not a one-for-one correspondence with Daniel's beast, but there is striking similarity. Daniel has *four* beasts with a total of seven heads; John's *one* Beast is seven-headed. John may be saying that his Beast is the embodiment of past evil powers in one monster. He may have pictured his Beast as being "an unholy hybrid" of Daniel's four beasts.[48]

These observations are important because they reveal the symbolic nature of John's Beast. In other words, John never intended his list of kings to be calculated in a linear, historical fashion, with each head of the Beast corresponding to an emperor. Therefore, we don't have to worry about which one is which head of the Beast. Perhaps the *seven* heads simply represent the fullness of evil, symbolizing the depths of Rome's depravity. Here's what scholar J. Nelson Kraybill suggests:

> Instead of taking John's enumeration of emperors too literally, however, we should understand the seven kings in more archetypal terms. The number "seven," in Revelation and in Hebrew tradition, symbolizes completion or fulfillment. It is likely that the five fallen kings represent all the deceased emperors, regardless of how we count them. The living emperor (17:10) may be Domitian, and the vision foresees yet another corrupt emperor to follow.[49]

However one decides to understand John's eight kings, we can be certain that they do refer to the Roman emperors of John's era. This seems clear from what we have learned so far. First, John references

---

47. Many scholars interpret Daniel's four beasts as representing four historical kingdoms that dominated Israel at some point in their history. Scholars often debate the exact identity of each kingdom.

48. DeSilva, *Discovering Revelation*, 130.

49. Kraybill, *Apocalypse and Allegiance*, 127.

Nero's suicide and return in Revelation 13:3, 12, 14. In doing so, second, John has built a rather pliable image of the Beast such that the language of "wounded" and "healed" can apply to both one of its heads and the entire Beast. This means that the one head of the Beast that was wounded (Nero) is at the same time an archetype for the Beast itself. In other words, Nero embodied the depraved essence of the Beast. Third, the Beast has throughout the vision been viewed in terms of the Roman Empire—its seven heads, for example, depict the seven hills of Rome, as well as her seven rulers. We can conclude, then, that the Beast is the Roman Empire as embodied through her despotic, egotistical emperors—the epitome of which was Nero.[50] And if John was writing during the reign of Domitian, he most certainly understood him as a Nero *redivivus*.

THE MARK: BUYING AND SELLING

Now that we have identified the Beast, we can finally revisit the mark of the Beast. John says that "no one can buy or sell unless he has the mark, that is, the name of the beast or the number of its name" (Rev 13:17). How does this connect with the Roman Empire and Rome's emperors?

As we learned above, Roman coins were one place the Beast's image could be found, and these images often made claims to deity and boastful blasphemies. If a person wanted to "buy or sell," it would be next to impossible to do so without using blasphemous coins to do so. As one scholar comments, "One could do little in commerce (13:17) without handling such a 'mark,' because allusions to the emperor's divinity appeared on many coins and even shipping bills and documents."[51]

The idea that "the mark" might have something to do with Roman imperial coinage has something going for it. Revelation, as we saw, associates the mark of the Beast with both the worship of the Beast

---

50. Thus, deSilva observes it was "John's conviction that Nero showed the world the Principate's truest colours" (*Discovering Revelation*, 149).

51. Keener, *Revelation*, 352.

and the image of the Beast (Rev 13:14–18; 14:9, 11; 16:2; 19:20; 20:4). That imperial coins were marked with deified images of the emperors makes it a good candidate for being one manifestation of the mark of the Beast.

It's also likely the mark has something to do with trade guilds. In the first century, many people participated in guilds for the same reason people do today—namely, for economic security and benefits. But like the Roman economy as a whole, trade guilds back then were deeply enmeshed in the worship of pagan deities and of the emperor. This fact made it hard for many people to steer clear of emperor worship. According to Kraybill, so close was the relationship between the imperial cult and trade guilds that there could even be crossover in leadership—one might be a priest of the imperial cult and patron of a guild.[52]

Members of a trade guild would have felt pressure to conform to cultic practices—or else risk losing their livelihood and economic security. However, Christians couldn't participate in these labor groups without compromising their faith. For example, membership in a trade guild might have been contingent on participating in its feasts, which likely entailed the worship of various deities and the emperor.[53] In light of this, it is easy to imagine how Christians would often have to forgo financial security in order to stay faithful to God.[54] That's why Kraybill's analysis is perhaps on the money when he says, "The emperor cult so pervaded commerce in the Roman world that it was difficult to buy or sell without the mark of the beast (13:17)."[55]

---

52. Kraybill, *Apocalypse and Allegiance*, 149 (see also 147).

53. Kraybill, *Apocalypse and Allegiance*, 162. He says, "Participating in meals that included worship of the gods or the emperor may have been required for membership in trade guilds or political associations. Abundant archaeological and literary evidence shows that trade guilds were present in the commercial city of Thyatira and elsewhere in cities of the New Testament. The guilds typically held ceremonial meals where relationships developed that enhanced business" (162). See also Keener, *Revelation*, 353; Gorman, *Reading Revelation*, 94.

54. See the discussion about Smyrna and Philadelphia, and "Jezebel" at Thyatira, in Kraybill, *Apocalypse and Allegiance*, 159–60 and 162, respectively.

55. Kraybill, *Apocalypse and Allegiance*, 149.

THE ROLE OF THE SECOND BEAST

Up until this point, we have focused on the first Beast of Revelation. But what about the second? If Rome is the first Beast that comes from the sea (Rev 13:1), then who is the second Beast that comes from the earth (Rev 13:11)? This second Beast has a particular task assigned to it—namely, it "makes the earth and its inhabitants worship the first beast" (Rev 13:12b). It employs "great signs" so that through them it "deceives those who dwell on earth, telling them to make an image for the beast that was wounded by the sword and yet lived" (13:14). This second Beast can even "give breath to the image of the beast, so that the image of the beast might even speak and might cause those who would not worship the image of the beast to be slain" (13:15). It also leads people to take the mark of the Beast for themselves (13:16–17). With whom, or what, in the first century Roman Empire might this second Beast be identified?

One clue might be in that elsewhere in Revelation, this second Beast is referred to as a "false prophet" (Rev 16:13; 19:20; 20:10). This is a good description for the second Beast because its task is to promote the worship of the first Beast. Its job is "religious" in nature.[56] This Beast also possesses the authority of the first Beast (Rev 13:12). The idea is that its work is approved and authorized by Rome. Some scholars think John might be referring to the institution of the imperial cult—especially the priests, who facilitated the worship of the emperors.[57] With respect to the province of Asia specifically, John's second Beast most likely refers to the *commune Asiae* (Asian Commune), which was the province's local governing institution that promoted the worship of the emperor and his family by setting up temples and images for them.[58]

---

56. "The beast has primarily a religious role since it is later repeatedly called 'the false prophet' (16:13; 19:20; 20:10)" (Beale, *Revelation*, 707).

57. So Witherington: "It is possible that John has in mind here someone specific, namely the asiarch, the high priest of the imperial cult" (*Revelation*, 184). See also Caird, *Revelation*, 171; Aune, *Revelation 6–16*, 756–57 (note especially Aune's comment on the office and function of an Asiarch on 756).

58. Caird, *Revelation*, 171–72. See also Aune, *Revelation 6–16*, 773–75. On the cities of Asia setting up temples for the worship of Caesar, see again ch. 3. With respect to John's claim that the

WHAT ABOUT TODAY?

It is interesting how the mark of the Beast has garnered cultlike attention in our culture. Out of the many important truths Revelation teaches, it is the mark-of-the-Beast passage that garners the most interest. Preachers have cautioned their congregants to be on the lookout for it, heaping speculation upon speculation about what it might be. Yet, strikingly, in many of these same sermons and discussions, the imperial cult is hardly ever discussed—even though it is an important part of Revelation's historical context. When I grew up hearing about the mark of the Beast, I never heard anything about the imperial cult even though such information is important for understanding that passage. That is why I have been at pains to point us back to that original context. As best as I can in a book such as this, I have led us back to John's world—his Caesar-worshiping, idol-loving, pagan-immersed world. In light of all that we have observed above, I think our observations lead us to four conclusions.

First, the mark of the Beast was a first-century phenomenon. For John, the mark had nothing to do with barcodes, vaccines, nanotechnology, Social Security numbers, or anything of the sort. None of these modern technological advancements would have been known to John or recognized by any of his readers. For John, the mark had to do with the Beast whose image was the object of worship. The *Beast* was a symbolic picture of the Roman Empire, whose blasphemy was embodied in *images* of the emperor, which was being *worshiped.* This makes sense given what we know about John's historical situation in Asia. It also makes sense of the earlier observation that Revelation was a letter that must have been discernible to its original readers.

For John, to *take the mark of the Beast* is simply another way of describing the person who desires to be a willing participant in Rome's blasphemous sociopolitical and economic way of life. To take the

---

Beast can perform "great signs" (Rev 13:13) and the image being able to "speak" (13:15), there is evidence from the ancient world that false teachers would attempt to deceive people by making images animate or at least appear to do so, and emperors were known to use magicians from time to time (Witherington, *Revelation*, 184). See also Keener, *Revelation*, 351–52.

mark is to align with—indeed, to *mark* oneself out as a collabora-tor in—the ways of empire. For Christians, who were sealed by the Lamb (Rev 7:1–4; 14:1), it was not an option to go along with Caesar or worship his image. Christians could not acquiesce to the blasphe-mous claims of Caesar. Christians were already worshipers of King Jesus, and there was not room for another lord.

Second, the mark is all about worship. Worship is the willful pledg-ing of allegiance to revere and deify another person or thing. It is to look on another with absolute devotion and loyalty. To receive the mark of the Beast, then, is an act of willful allegiance. It is to identify oneself with the ways of the Beast. The mark is an identity *mark*-er. It makes public one's association with the forces of darkness. Like we saw in the letter from Pliny to the emperor Trajan, the worship of the emperor's image was a public test to show where one's alle-giances truly were. That's why Christians should never fear acciden-tally taking the mark of the Beast. The mark is a willful—and hence nonaccidental—act of worship.

Third, the mark of the Beast is most fundamentally not a physical reality. As we saw above, Revelation's mark of the Beast is situated opposite of the seal of the Lamb. This seal does not at all appear to be physi-cal like, say, a tattoo or other visible markers. Like Ezekiel's mark on the righteous, the seal of the Lamb in Revelation is probably unseen to the naked eye. It's a *spiritual* marker, not a physical one. The same must be said about its sinister counterpart—the mark of the Beast. John uses the "mark" only in a symbolic sense. This does not mean, of course, that the mark cannot have physical manifestations. Christians, for example, have the inner work of the Spirit visibly manifested in their actions (Gal 5:22–25). Similarly, those with evil hearts manifest evil in the world by their wicked deeds (Gal 5:19–21). The invisible mark of the Beast can also have physical manifestations—most nota-bly in coins and statues of the emperor. Roman coins displayed visi-bly the blasphemous beliefs of the imperial cult. The imperial statues, temples, and coins symbolized, and hence publicly communicated, the propaganda of an empire bent on violence and evil.

Could there be manifestations today of something like a mark of the Beast? *Yes.* Revelation's Beast is not merely the Rome (or Nero) of John's time. It is a symbol of blasphemy and rebellion against the ways of the Lamb. Today, Revelation's Beast continues to be a symbol for *anything* and *anyone* that exalts itself in the place of Christ. The Beast can even serve as a paradigm for how we understand the future Antichrist (the subject of a later chapter). The Beast also illustrates the seductive nature of the various antichrists that have existed in the past and continue to exist today.

Throughout history, beastly leaders and institutions have emerged, destroying lives and bringing suffering. These modern beasts also have "marks" that symbolize their violence and blasphemy. One cannot help but think of the icons of racism such as the KKK hood and the burning of crosses. The emblems of uber-nationalism (such as the Nazis' swastika) and communism (such as the hammer and sickle of the Soviet Union) both embody beastly evils. The Beast— typified by the wealth and excess of Babylon—can also be found in the symbols of unrestrained capitalism. Many of the comforts of the Western world have been made possible by the greed of international corporations. These institutions can sell goods and services so cheaply because the products themselves were made in sweatshop factories in the majority world—all for the benefit and comfort of the Western world. When an empire's wealth and power is made possible by the abuse of workers and by violating basic human rights, the icons of that empire are tainted, corrupt—indeed, *marked* out—as beastly in character. For those of us who live in the luxuries of the West, we need to ask how we can bear the seal of the Lamb in a land filled with the iconography of the Beast. We need to commit ourselves to rethink our own role in society as we, too, confront the propaganda of empire.

These questions are important because as Christians, we are *not* called to escape this world but rather to participate in its renewal. Our ultimate calling, after all, is to pray "Your kingdom come" (Matt 6:10). Sometimes we must do this in the face of persecution. We may be called to bear witness to the Lamb in the face of all the beastly manifestations of our age—no matter where, or when, we live. We are not escapists. It is not God's plan to vacuum us up before trials and tribulations occur. Like the seven churches before us, we are called to make our testimony of Christ's authority public. Revelation does not teach that we will be spared from trials or tribulations. It does not teach that we will be sucked up into heaven so that we can be spared seasons of difficulty. Yet, this is what many Christians continue to believe. But, in fact, this isn't taught in Revelation. In fact, as we will see in the next chapter, it's taught nowhere in the entire Bible.

4

WILL CHRISTIANS BE RAPTURED?

At the heart of the Christian hope is the return of Christ. This hope has long been captured in the Apostles' Creed: "He ascended into heaven, and sitteth on the right hand of God the Father almighty. From thence he shall come to judge the quick and the dead." Even though all Christians believe in the return of Christ, not everyone agrees on how it will pan out. Many believe Christ's second coming will happen in two parts: the first part is what has come to be called the "rapture," and the second part is Christ's actual return.

The basic idea goes like this. Jesus will return at a time when nobody expects. As Tim LaHaye and Jerry Jenkins describe it, "One of the chief characteristics of the Rapture of the church is that it will be sudden, unexpected, and will catch people by surprise."[1] When the rapture does happen, it will be done secretly, without noise or fanfare—a covert operation of sorts. The rapture will draw Christians out of the world and into the clouds, whisking them quickly into heaven. Hal Lindsey refers to it as "Evacuation Time."[2] John Hagee describes it as being "snatched away."[3] The rapture, exclaims Hagee, is "the only way to fly!"[4]

---

1. LaHaye and Jenkins, *End Times*, 139. LaHaye and Jenkins speak of the rapture as a "secret" event (126). See also Hal Lindsey, *Planet Earth—2000 A.D. Will Mankind Survive?* (Palos Verdes, CA: Western Front, 1994), 285.

2. Lindsey, *Planet Earth*, 285.

3. John Hagee, *Beginning of the End: The Assassination of Yitzhak Rabin and the Coming Antichrist* (Nashville: Thomas Nelson, 1996), 106. Lindsey likewise describes it as being "snatched away" (*Planet Earth*, 288).

4. Hagee, *Beginning of the End*, 105.

Here's how it fits into the larger scheme of events. After the rapture, the earth will undergo an awful tribulation at the hand of the Antichrist. He and his sinister forces will wreak havoc on the earth. The Antichrist's dominion will come to a swift end, however, when Jesus returns *once more* with his saints to launch his millennial (thousand-year) kingdom. Even though this return would technically be Jesus's *third* coming, most rapture believers still refer to this as his "second coming."[5] The rapture is seen as a second coming that isn't a true *second* coming. Jesus only comes to the clouds. He never actually sets foot on the ground.

Belief in the rapture has dominated much of the American evangelical landscape for the better part of the last century. In the circles I grew up in, everyone talked about the rapture. Pastors warned about it, revival meetings were focused on it, and believers (anxiously) anticipated it. Everyone who didn't want to be left behind to go through the tribulation was encouraged to prepare for their imminent exit from earth. So engrained is the idea of rapture in evangelicalism that some pastors have even left prewritten messages to those who will be left behind.[6]

For some, the rapture is a nonnegotiable fact of Christian dogma. According to Hagee, for example, to deny the rapture is itself a sign of the times. Citing Peter's warning that "scoffers" will rise up in the "last days" (2 Pet 3:3), Hagee says, "The simple fact that we hear voices denying the certainty of a literal Rapture is, in and of itself, another sign that we are the terminal generation."[7]

Rapture theology received a big boost in popularity in the mid-nineties with the publication of the Left Behind book series.

---

5. See, e.g., John MacArthur, *John 12–21* (Chicago: Moody, 2008), 101–2; see also Lindsey, *Planet Earth*, 286.

6. In his book *Beginning of the End*, John Hagee anticipates that some of his future readers will consist of those who have missed the rapture. He thus offers a word of encouragement "to the one who finds this book in the future time of tribulation" (xi).

7. Hagee, *Beginning of the End*, 101. Hagee laments further: "Many evangelical churches have preached the doctrine of the Rapture for years, but now even they are under attack for teaching that a literal gathering of the church will occur. More liberal theologians are even shouting in chorus, 'There will never be a rapture!'" (*Beginning of the End*, 103).

For many pastors, and especially youth leaders, these novels inspired soul-wrenching sermons. With the very mention of the word "rapture," you could easily frighten someone into accepting Christ. One never knew, after all, when it would occur. Who in their right mind would want to be left behind to experience the wrath of the Antichrist? Not me. Growing up in those days, we were all encouraged to be "rapture ready." We were warned: *The rapture is going to happen, and you don't want to be left behind.* As a teenager, I especially took that message to heart.

But some Christians question whether the idea of a rapture is found in the Bible. In their opinion, the scriptural passages that are cited in support of rapture theology are not as rock solid as many people assume. In fact, they say, many of the assumptions that rapture theology is built on are quite wobbly.

So, let's ask: *Does the Bible teach there will be a rapture?* Many Christians have perhaps never stopped to ask that simple question. The belief in a rapture is so enmeshed into the DNA of some Christian traditions that the question itself might even appear heretical. But let's reassure ourselves. It's never wrong to ask questions, and it's never wrong to examine our assumptions in the light of the Bible. So let's test rapture theology, placing it side-by-side with Scripture to see whether they line up.

THE ASSUMPTIONS BEHIND THE RAPTURE

Some versions of rapture theology are based on the idea that God will spare Christians from going through the tribulation. This is known as the *pretribulational rapture*. This view says believers will be raptured away from the earth to enjoy a time of comfort in the heavenly realm. Believers will spend their time participating in a celebratory feast known as the marriage supper of the Lamb and being rewarded for their service to Christ. Spared from all the bad stuff, these saints will be tucked safely away in heaven while all the nightmares rage on the earth below. Some of those left behind will choose to become

Christians during this time of tribulation, but many will not. Either way, life will be rough for everyone. That's why it's important to be ready for the rapture, so that you can be spared from the coming trials.

LaHaye and Jenkins are one example of an argument for a pretribulational rapture. They base their argument on a range of passages. One is Revelation 3:10, which says: "Because you have kept my word about patient endurance, I will keep you from the hour of trial that is coming on the whole world, to try those who dwell on the earth." LaHaye and Jenkins put a lot of stock in this verse, describing it as "one of the best promises guaranteeing the church's rapture before the Tribulation."[8]

But does this verse teach a pretribulational rapture? After all, the rapture is nowhere mentioned in—or near—this verse. The next verse does record Jesus saying he is "coming soon" (Rev 3:11). But there's nothing in this passage that requires us to think it speaks of a rapture as the first of a two-part return of Christ. It could simply refer to Jesus's second coming as a one-time event. So, what makes LaHaye and Jenkins think it refers to the rapture?

What drives their interpretation is the assumption that each of the seven churches mentioned in Revelation 2–3 represents a different period in church history. For them, the Philadelphian church represents the era of the church, which started around 1750 and will last until the rapture.[9] In his commentary on Revelation, LaHaye charts it like this:[10]

1. **AD 30–100:** "The Apostolic Church"—Ephesus (Rev 2:1–7)

2. **AD 100–312:** "The Persecuted Church"—Smyrna (Rev 2:8–11)

---

8. LaHaye and Jenkins, *End Times*, 130.

9. LaHaye and Jenkins, *End Times*, 130–32 (see also 80). They write: "The message of Christ to the church at Philadelphia was not only for that little church but also to the 'open door' church—that is, the evangelistic, missionary-minded church, which started about 1750 and will exist right up to the time Christ comes to rapture His church" (130).

10. The following is based on the chart given in Tim LaHaye, *Revelation Unveiled*, rev. and updated (Grand Rapids: Zondervan, 1999), 24.

3. **AD 312–606:** "The Indulged Church"—Pergamum (Rev 2:12–17)

4. **AD 606–Tribulation:** "The Pagan Church"—Thyatira (Rev 2:18–29)

5. **AD 1520–Tribulation:** "The Dead Church"—Sardis (Rev 3:1–6)

6. **AD 1750–Rapture:** "The Church Christ Loved"— Philadelphia (Rev 3:7–13)

7. **AD 1900–Tribulation:** "The Lukewarm Church"— Laodicea (Rev 3:14–22)

This means that the messages given to John were not merely messages for the first-century churches of Asia. They were also *prophecies* about future eras of history. LaHaye explains things further, saying,

> It should be kept in mind that the first three church ages differ from the last four in that each of the former stopped at the beginning of the next church. Ephesus was replaced by Smyrna, Smyrna by Pergamum, and Pergamum by Thyatira ... [but] we have Thyatira, Sardis, and Philadelphia with us at the present time. Thus Laodicea adds to this church age by arising from the three that preceded it.[11]

For LaHaye and Jenkins, the message to the Philadelphian church is not ultimately a message that concerns the first-century Philadelphians, but rather those believers who live in the sixth era of church history. This is how they get rapture theology out of Revelation 3:10. When Christ says he will preserve *Philadelphia* "from the hour of trial that is coming on the whole world," he is ultimately referring to the rapture of those professing Christians living in the modern era.[12]

---

11. LaHaye, *Revelation*, 84–85.
12. See the discussion in LaHaye and Jenkins, *End Times*, 130–31.

But not every professing Christian will get raptured. Some are fake Christians. As you can see from the chart above, Philadelphia isn't the only church era currently in existence. There's also Thyatira, Sardis, and Laodicea. These churches represent, respectively, those believers who are "pagan," "dead," and "lukewarm." Those churches are *not* promised rapture, for they continue through the rapture and into the tribulation.[13] Only Philadelphia is promised escape (Rev 3:10).

Philadelphia must represent the final church era that is raptured because, argues LaHaye, the world has yet to experience a world-wide tribulation that the text talks about.[14] He says it is clear that "the church of Philadelphia has end-time significance, for it is referred to as 'alive' during the last days."[15] That is, LaHaye thinks that when Jesus tells the Philadelphians he is "coming soon," this implies the church will be around at that time.[16] Since the Philadelphians will be *spared* from the tribulation, this must mean they will be taken out of the picture. And since Jesus tells them he is coming soon, the way they are spared must be through his coming. But this can't refer to the final coming of Jesus. Why? Because Jesus is coming to take the church *from* an earth that has trouble coming upon it. In other words, a time of trouble is coming to the earth, not Jesus's peaceful kingdom. This second coming, therefore, must be a different sort of coming—a

---

13. Speaking of Thyatira, LaHaye says: "Our Lord here predicts that this church and those that are persuaded to follow her [Jezebel, who for LaHaye represents the Roman Catholic Church] false teachings will go into the Great Tribulation, when she will, according to Revelation 17, be the Church of the Tribulation" (*Revelation*, 70). LaHaye goes on to describe Sardis (which for him represents the Reformation church) as a largely dead church that needs to get right with God before it's too late; some in Sardis, he says, are faithful (see 72–77). He describes Laodicea as those confessing Christians who are "apostate" and in danger of damnation (85, 87). As I understand LaHaye, Christians today fall under any of the churches: Thyatira, Sardis, Philadelphia, or Laodicea. The ones who resemble the church of Philadelphia will be kept from the tribulation. For, according to LaHaye, only that church was promised it (Rev 3:10).

14. LaHaye, *Revelation*, 81.

15. LaHaye and Jenkins, *End Times*, 131.

16. Commenting on the exhortation given to Philadelphia in 3:11 ("I am coming soon. Hold fast what you have, so that no one may seize your crown"), LaHaye says, "Our Lord's counsel to the church of Philadelphia is based on the promise of His second coming. It is interesting to note that the challenge is made on the basis that the church of Philadelphia will be in existence at His coming" (*Revelation*, 82).

secret coming *for* his church to help them escape *from* earth's coming demise. Hence, *rapture*.

LaHaye and Jenkins assume that the "trial" mentioned in Revelation 3:10 is a final, end-time "great tribulation."[17] They also reference 1 Thessalonians 1:10 and 5:9. These verses describe how Christians will be spared from "wrath." LaHaye and Jenkins then equate "wrath" with "the Tribulation." They conclude: "Since the Tribulation is *especially* the time of God's wrath, and since Christians are not appointed to wrath, then it follows that the church will be raptured *before* the Tribulation."[18]

I'll say more about their interpretation of these texts in a moment, but at this point, it's easy to see why Revelation 3:10 is so important for their view. If God has promised the Philadelphian church that they will be delivered from the coming "trial" (the *great tribulation*), and if the Philadelphian church represents a future era of believers who exist before that trial, then it follows that God must rescue them in some way to cause them to *skip* the tribulation the rest of earth's population must endure. The conclusion, according to LaHaye and Jenkins, is that believers skip the tribulation *by way of a rapture*.

That is the logic behind the pretribulational rapture. But before we adopt this viewpoint, we need to ask three important questions.

DO THE SEVEN CHURCHES REPRESENT SEVEN PERIODS OF CHURCH HISTORY?

This idea that the seven churches of Revelation represent seven ages of church history is popular among modern prophecy teachers.[19] But when we dive deeper, we notice some issues. The first is that church history is simply too diverse for it to accommodate this sort of generalization.[20] Second, it would mean that most Christians throughout

---

17. LaHaye and Jenkins, *End Times*, 131. Here, they get "great tribulation" from Matt 24.

18. LaHaye and Jenkins, *End Times*, 132–34, emphasis original.

19. See, e.g., Matt Hagee, *Your Guide to the Apocalypse: What You Should Know before the World Comes to an End* (Colorado Springs: WaterBrook, 2017), 113–14, 148, 163–64, 184.

20. Keener rightly calls it a "forced reading of church history" (*Revelation*, 75).

history (especially those in the first three eras) were wrong to anticipate the return of Jesus in their own lifetimes. As New Testament
scholar Craig Keener says,

> If Revelation requires the completion of seven church ages
> before Jesus' return, then in most centuries of church history
> Christians had no right to expect the imminent return of the
> Lord! This would be a curious conclusion for advocates of the
> seven church ages view, most of whom vehemently emphasize
> the imminence of Christ's return.[21]

Keener is on to something. After all, LaHaye's final age (Laodicea)
doesn't even start until 1900.

A third problem is that the association of Revelation's churches with
periods of church history is, as David deSilva says, "starkly Eurocentric."
It effectively ignores "the state of the Church in the southern hemisphere and the Middle and Far East throughout this history."[22]

In short, the problem with the idea that seven churches represent
seven periods of church history is that it requires a very flat, one-
dimensional view of church history. The entire global church through
the past two thousand years cannot be squeezed into such simplistic
categories. There's just too much diversity in the body of Christ to
do such a thing.

WHAT WAS PHILADELPHIA PROMISED?

Another big question with regard to the church-age theory is how
it understands Jesus's promise to "keep" the Philadelphian church
"from the hour of trial" (Rev 3:10). But why is this taken to refer
to the final tribulation? Can't it simply be a promise to the local
Philadelphian church that they will be preserved through—and not
be taken out of—an upcoming season of difficulty?[23] LaHaye and

---

21. Keener, *Revelation*, 75.
22. DeSilva, *Discovering Revelation*, 70; see also 71.
23. See Aune, *Revelation 1–5*, 240.

John MacArthur object to this idea by pointing to the Greek word *ek* ("from" or "out") that occurs in this verse. This means, they argue, that Jesus promises to take Christians *from* the trial by rapturing them *out of* this world.[24]

But does this objection work? Read again what Jesus tells the Philadelphians: "I will keep you from [*ek*] the hour of trial" (Rev 3:10). Notice that Jesus is not saying he will keep Christians from the world, but from a *situation* that is going to happen in the world. This is very similar to Jesus's prayer in John 17:15, where he prays for his followers to be preserved in the world: "I do not ask that you take them out of [*ek*] the world, but that you *keep them from* [*ek*] the evil one."[25] This seems to be what Jesus has in mind for the Philadelphians, too. If so, it would make sense of the next verse, where Jesus encourages them to stay faithful until the end (Rev 3:11).[26]

Both LaHaye and MacArthur put a lot of stock in how the verse says this trial "is coming *on the whole world*" (Rev 3:10).[27] But I don't think this is enough to support their case that the trial must be a *global* one. While it is true that terms such as "world" (*oikoumenē*) and "whole world" (*oikoumenēs holēs*) can mean the world in its entirety (see Rev 12:9), New Testament writers often use the same or similar expressions to refer to small and local regions on the earth.[28]

For example, Luke reports that "a decree went out from Caesar Augustus that *all the world* [*pasan tēn oikoumenēn*] should be registered" (Luke 2:1). Clearly, Luke did not intend to include the Chinese or the native North Americans, but only people living in the Roman

---

24. See, e.g., LaHaye and Jenkins, *End Times*, 131; John MacArthur, *Because the Time Is Near* (Chicago: Moody, 2007), 93.

25. Emphasis added. According to Aune, outside Rev 3:10, the only other place in Greek literature where *tēreō ek* ("I will keep from") is found is in John 17:15 (*Revelation 1–5*, 239). See also Keener, *Revelation*, 154; Beale, *Revelation*, 290–92.

26. The Philadelphians must persevere or be excluded from the kingdom; see Keener, *Revelation*, 151.

27. See LaHaye, *Revelation*, 81; LaHaye and Jenkins, *End Times*, 130–31; MacArthur, *Because the Time Is Near*, 93.

28. This insight and the following examples come from Beale, *Revelation*, 290.

Empire. Similarly, in Acts 11:28, Luke reports how Agabus prophesied there would be a "great famine over *all the world* [*holēn tēn oikoumenēn*]." The famine occurred, he says, during the reign of the emperor Claudius (11:28). There is no reason to think, nor is there external evidence to suggest, that there was a worldwide famine that hit every continent during this time. I could give other examples, but this is enough to show that the trial mentioned in Revelation 3:10 cannot be said to be universal *just because* the text describes it as "coming on the whole world." Most likely, it simply refers to a very trying season that will come on the seven churches—a situation through which the Philadelphian believers will be preserved. There is, of course, a valuable point of application in this verse for all Christians in all times and locations: stay faithful to Jesus through every trial, and he will preserve you in his peace (John 16:33).[29]

WHAT ARE THE BEST PASSAGES THAT TEACH THE RAPTURE?

I mentioned earlier how LaHaye and Jenkins look to passages such as 1 Thessalonians 1:10 and 5:9 to argue that Christians will be spared from "wrath" when Jesus returns, which they take to mean "tribulation." But why should we think "wrath" here refers to a seven-year tribulation? In fact, the context seems to suggest that Christians will be spared from the final judgment, not tribulation.[30] Christians are spared *not* because they will be raptured, but because they are in Christ and hence forgiven of their sins. The entire context seems to point to judgment following the return of Christ, not a secret rapture.

So, what motivates LaHaye and Jenkins to think these verses refer to the rapture? Part of the reason, it seems, is how close they are to 1 Thessalonians 4:13–18, a passage they consider to be foundational for

---

29. So Beale, *Revelation*, 291.

30. So Michael L. Brown and Craig S. Keener, *Not Afraid of the Antichrist: Why We Don't Believe in a Pre-tribulational Rapture* (Minneapolis: Chosen, 2019), 123–26 (see esp. 125–26).

rapture theology.[31] In fact, they say this passage (specifically 4:16–17) is one of the "best passages" that teaches the rapture—along with John 14:1–3 and 1 Corinthians 15:50–58.[32] Let's examine each of these passages to see what exactly they teach.

1 THESSALONIANS 4:13-18

This passage is one that believers in the rapture tend to cite the most when making arguments for their position.[33] Here is the passage:

> But we do not want you to be uninformed, brothers, about those who are asleep, that you may not grieve as others do who have no hope. For since we believe that Jesus died and rose again, even so, through Jesus, God will bring with him those who have fallen asleep. For this we declare to you by a word from the Lord, that we who are alive, who are left until the *coming* [*parousia*] of the Lord, will not precede those who have fallen asleep. For the Lord himself will descend from heaven with a cry of command, with the voice of an archangel, and with the sound of the trumpet of God. And the dead in Christ will rise first. Then we who are alive, who are left, will be *caught up* [*harpazō*] together with them in the clouds to *meet* [*apantēsis*] the Lord in the air, and so we will always be with the Lord. Therefore encourage one another with these words. (1 Thess 4:13–18)

---

31. See LaHaye and Jenkins, *End Times*, 132–33. Though they do not explicitly cite 1 Thess 4:13–18, it's clear they have it in mind (see esp. 132). Note also how in these pages they refer to the *content* of that passage often and the integral role it plays in their interpretations of 1 Thess 1:10; 5:9. On this, see also 122–24.

32. LaHaye and Jenkins, *End Times*, 122. See also MacArthur, *John 12–21*, 101. In his commentary, LaHaye also thinks Rev 4:1 refers to the rapture (*Revelation*, 99–101). This is where John, who LaHaye thinks "represents the Church," is called up to heaven by Jesus: "Come up here, and I will show you what must take place after this" (Rev 4:1; LaHaye, *Revelation*, 100). A lot of LaHaye's reasoning is due to his assumption that Rev 6–18 refers exclusively to a future tribulation. And because he doesn't think the church will take part in the tribulation, Rev 4:1 makes perfect sense as a rapture text (see esp. p. 100). I will address this understanding of Rev 6–18 in the next chapter.

33. See, e.g., Hagee, *Beginning of the End*, 101.

Hal Lindsey says this passage is "a detailed account of the Rapture."[34] Is this true? To find out, we need to pay close attention to three Greek words that appear in the text: *parousia, harpazō,* and *apantēsis.*

Parousia is translated above as "coming" (4:15). But this doesn't do justice to the word. Strictly speaking, the word could best be translated as *presencing.*[35] Of course, parousia can entail "coming," which is why many translations opt for it. That said, parousia focuses more on the *person* who is coming than on the *event* of the coming itself. An example of this comes from early Greek culture, where parousia was used to describe the arrival of a king or political dignitary to a city. The arrival elicited a jubilant response on behalf of the citizens, who bestowed various honors on the king as they welcomed him.[36] Most likely, this is also how the Greek-speaking Thessalonians would have understood Paul's use of parousia—namely, as the arrival of King Jesus.[37]

The same can be said about 4:17, where Paul says believers will "meet the Lord in the air." The word "meet," *apantēsis,* is another word from the ancient world that was used to depict "a civic custom of antiquity whereby a public welcome was accorded by a city to important visitors."[38] This would mean that believers are only "caught up" (*harpazō*) from the earth and taken "in the clouds to meet [*apantēsis*] the Lord in the air" *so they can immediately welcome him back to the earth.*

So, when Paul talks about "the coming of the Lord" and how believers will "meet the Lord in the air," he doesn't seem to be talking about

---

34. Lindsey, *Planet Earth,* 287.

35. As N. T. Wright says, "This [*parousia*] is usually translated as 'coming,' but literally it means 'presence'—that is, presence as opposed to absence." Wright, *Surprised by Hope: Rethinking Heaven, the Resurrection, and the Mission of the Church* (New York: HarperOne, 2008), 128.

36. Albrecht Oepke, "Παρουσία, Πάρειμι," *TDNT* 5:859–60. See also Wright, who, in addition to highlighting the word's Greco-Roman context, also emphasizes the Jewish background and usage (*Surprised by Hope,* 129–30).

37. Abraham J. Malherbe, *The Letters to the Thessalonians,* AB (New York: Doubleday, 2000), 272.

38. Erik Peterson, "Ἀπάντησις," *TDNT* 1:380.

Jesus taking people from the earth. What he *is* talking about is the Lord's coming to the earth and being welcomed by his followers in order to take up residence among them. As biblical scholar N. T. Wright says,

> When Paul speaks of "meeting" the Lord "in the air," the point is precisely not—as in the popular rapture theology—that the saved believers would then stay up in the air somewhere, away from earth. The point is that, having gone out to meet their returning Lord, they will escort him royally into his domain, that is, back to the place they have come from.[39]

In other words, Paul is not talking about Christians leaving earth, but Jesus's coming to earth. And as the ancient context suggests, this welcoming of the king is hardly a secret event—but rather one of much fanfare and celebration. That's why we shouldn't take it to mean anything like "rapture" in the popular sense of the term. If we think like Paul's first readers, this is the conclusion we should draw. Paul was using the imagery of his time, not ours. If we want to understand his ancient letter to the Thessalonians, we need to think like a Thessalonian: *when the King comes, we will go out of the city to welcome him in order to escort him back to it.*

JOHN 14:1-3

In this passage, Jesus offers words of encouragement to his disciples. He comforts them because his imminent departure will leave them saddened. He reassures them, saying,

> Let not your hearts be troubled. Believe in God; believe also in me. In my Father's house are many rooms. If it were not so, would I have told you that I go to prepare a place for you? And if I go and prepare a place for you, I will come again and will take you to myself, that where I am you may be also. (John 14:1-3)

---

39. Wright, *Surprised by Hope*, 133. Regarding Paul's talk of being caught up in the air, see Wright's discussion on 132–33, especially where Wright goes on to add that "this is highly charged metaphor, not literal description" (133).

Many people interpret "I will come again" and "take you to myself" to be a reference to the rapture, not the second coming. MacArthur, for example, insists this passage must refer to the rapture. This, he says, is because it lacks any discussion about judgment—an event the Bible often associates with the second coming.[40] MacArthur also points out how this text never mentions angels gathering believers like Matthew 24:30–31, which he thinks refers to the second coming. That passage, says MacArthur, is different from John 14:2–3, which only mentions how Jesus himself will "personally come for them." MacArthur also observes how the passage says nothing about believers coming back *with* Christ, but only that he will come *for* them. Because other second coming texts speak of the saints returning with Christ, MacArthur thinks John 14:2–3 must be a reference to a different sort of coming—namely, the rapture.[41]

But there seem to be multiple problems with this interpretation. For starters, the argument is based largely on silence. Just because John 14:1–3 doesn't mention anything about judgment should not lead us to conclude this text has nothing to do with the second coming. Perhaps Jesus never mentions judgment in that passage because it was not relevant to what he wanted to do in the context, which was to comfort grieving disciples.

Interestingly, MacArthur's argument actually works against him. For example, recall from above how MacArthur cites Matthew 24:30–31 as a second coming text. But nowhere in that passage does it mention anything about the saints coming *with* Jesus. It only speaks of Jesus coming *for* his elect through his angels. But if John 14:1–3 cannot be taken as a second coming text on the grounds that it fails to mention anything about the saints coming with Christ, then MacArthur should not take Matthew 24:30–31 as a second coming text for the same reason. Given the interpretive logic MacArthur employs, it's

---

40. MacArthur, *John 12–21*, 101–2.

41. MacArthur, *John 12–21*, 102. He cites Rev 19:8, 14 as an example of the saints returning with Christ.

also odd that he would interpret John 14:2–3 as a rapture passage. Nowhere, after all, does this passage mention anything about the voice of an archangel or a trumpet blasting. Yet these are the very things depicted in 1 Thessalonians 4:13–18, a passage MacArthur cites in support of rapture theology.[42]

So, what's going on in John 14:1–3? When Jesus says, "I will come again," he is referring not to a secret rapture but to his visible and very public second coming (14:3). When he says he "will take you to myself," he doesn't mean he will take believers from the earth. He simply means that when he appears, his disciples will be with him again. The emphasis is not on their leaving anything—much less leaving earth. Rather, it's on their *being with Jesus where he is.* This is exactly what he tells them: "And if I go and prepare a place for you, I will come again and will take you to myself, that *where I am you may be also*" (14:3).

I can imagine someone pushing back a little on this, saying, "Yes, but Jesus is preparing a place for his disciples in heaven, and that's the context for his coming. His goal, therefore, must be to bring them back to heaven, to the place he has prepared for them."[43] But that is reading the text through the wrong lens. In fact, when we consider Revelation 21:1–4, we see that the ultimate aim of Jesus's return is not to take people from earth to heaven, but to bring heaven to earth. What he is preparing is not a home in heaven, but a reunited heaven and earth:

> Then I saw a new heaven and a new earth, for the first heaven and the first earth had passed away, and the sea was no more. And I saw the holy city, new Jerusalem, coming down out of heaven from God, prepared as a bride adorned for her husband. And I heard a loud voice from the throne saying, "Behold, the dwelling place of God is with man. He will dwell with them, and they will be his people, and God himself will be with them as their God.

---

42. See MacArthur, *John 12–21*, 101–2; see also MacArthur, *Because the Time Is Near*, 16, 93, 287.

43. Lindsey, in the context of citing John 14:1–4, says, "We are snatched away before we even know what hit us. We are then taken directly to His Father's House where he has already prepared a place for us" (*Planet Earth*, 288).

> He will wipe away every tear from their eyes, and death shall be
> no more, neither shall there be mourning, nor crying, nor pain
> anymore, for the former things have passed away."

This text says three important things: (1) heaven is coming to the earth, (2) God's dwelling place will be with humanity, and (3) Christ's return will console our grief and wipe tears away. This is similar to Jesus's message to the disciples in John 14. He promises (1) to return to the earth and (2) to be reunited with his disciples, and (3) he depicts this event as a source of comfort.

This should also remind us of 1 Thessalonians 4:17. There Paul says, "Then we who are alive, who are left, will be caught up together with them in the clouds to meet the Lord in the air, *and so we will always be with the Lord.*" As we saw above, this passage does not teach a secret rapture. It simply teaches the second coming. The saints will meet the Lord in the air and escort him back to the earth, where he will rule and reign. It is in this context that the saints "will always be with the Lord." The point is the same as John 14:3. When Jesus returns, his disciples will always be with him. That is the sense in which Jesus says, "I will come again and will take you to myself." The emphasis is not on Jesus *taking* us from, or to, any place, but rather *personally receiving us* so that we can be with him for all eternity—wherever he is. And where will he be? As the historical context of 1 Thessalonians 4:13–18 suggests, and as the text of Revelation 21:1–4 attests, the King is coming to the earth to set up his kingdom. Like every dignitary in the ancient world, he will be received with celebration and joy by the citizens of his kingdom. *That* is what gives us joy and hope as we wait for him.

1 CORINTHIANS 15:50-58

This is the final go-to passage for those who believe in the rapture.[44] Does this text teach that God will whisk believers from the earth? Or is it teaching what the other passages above do, namely that God is not taking people from the earth but renewing them within it?

---

44. See, e.g., Hagee, *Beginning of the End*, 102–3; Lindsey, *Planet Earth*, 286.

The entirety of 1 Corinthians 15 is about the resurrection. By "resurrection," Paul means the *physical* and *bodily* rising from the dead. He is not talking about a *spiritual* resurrection in the sense of going to heaven when we die. To the contrary, Paul operates much closer to earth than that. He begins the chapter with a word of encouragement for believers to maintain their faith. He also speaks about the resurrection of Christ—specifically about those who witnessed it (1 Cor 15:1–11). He adds that Christ's resurrection is nonnegotiable. It is the core of the Christian faith itself (15:12–19). The resurrection of Christ makes possible and comes before the resurrection of the saints (15:20–23). Because Jesus has been raised, so too will the believer. Christ is described as the "firstfruits," as a *preview*, of what is coming for all the saints (15:23a). When will "those who belong to Christ" be resurrected? Paul is clear: *when Christ returns* (15:23b). What happens next? *The end happens.* When Christ returns, the saints will be resurrected, Christ will consummate his rule and defeat his enemies, and God's presence will envelop all creation (15:24–28). This is *the end*. It's the consummation of all things.

Paul does not provide a detailed blueprint for how it's all going to happen. And that's a point we must remember: nothing here talks about how the second coming happens. There's nothing about a two-step process for the second coming—about a rapture whisking away believers for several years that is later followed by Christ's return. Paul simply says the second coming kicks off the resurrection of the believers, which is followed by Christ's victory over his enemies. The text simply tells us *that* all this happens, not *how* it happens.

Paul closes this section with a brief discussion about the centrality of the resurrection to the church's faith and practice, along with his own personal devotion to the doctrine (15:29–34). This is followed by extended comments on the nature and mechanics of the bodily resurrection (15:35–49). This passage need not detain us other than to say that Paul is here continuing his discussion about *physical* and *bodily* resurrection. This brings us to our passage, namely, 1 Corinthians 15:50–58. Here's the text in full:

I tell you this, brothers: flesh and blood cannot inherit the
kingdom of God, nor does the perishable inherit the imperishable. Behold! I tell you a mystery. We shall not all sleep, but
we shall all be changed, in a moment, in the twinkling of an
eye, at the last trumpet. For the trumpet will sound, and the
dead will be raised imperishable, and we shall be changed. For
this perishable body must put on the imperishable, and this
mortal body must put on immortality. When the perishable
puts on the imperishable, and the mortal puts on immortality,
then shall come to pass the saying that is written:

"Death is swallowed up in victory."

"O death, where is your victory?
    O death, where is your sting?"

The sting of death is sin, and the power of sin is the law. But
thanks be to God, who gives us the victory through our Lord
Jesus Christ.

Therefore, my beloved brothers, be steadfast, immovable,
always abounding in the work of the Lord, knowing that in
the Lord your labor is not in vain.

The first thing to notice is how similar it is to 1 Thessalonians 4:13–
18. Both texts discuss the rising of those who *sleep*, the resurrection
of those who are *dead*, and the sound of the *trumpet* (1 Cor 15:51–
52; 1 Thess 4:13–16). It's reasonable to conclude, then, that these
two passages speak about the same event.[45] So, if I am correct that
1 Thessalonians 4:13–18 is not about the rapture, then 1 Corinthians
15:50–58 cannot be about the rapture either.

If we were to ignore 1 Corinthians 15:50–58 and simply read the
rest of chapter 15, we would walk away without any notion of a rapture. This is because Paul's focus is on an earthly resurrection, not a

---

45. Wright reaches the same conclusion (see *Surprised by Hope*, 131).

trip to heaven. In fact, nowhere in the whole chapter does Paul talk about Christians leaving the earth. It's all about renewed life on earth. When Paul says, "Flesh and blood cannot inherit the kingdom of God," he is not suggesting believers should hope to leave behind bodily life on earth and exchange it for a home in heaven. For Paul, "flesh" (*sarx*) often carries negative connotations such as sinfulness, worldliness, and the overall corruption that pervades mortal humanity.[46] That's why the phrase "flesh and blood" most likely means something along those same lines—namely, human existence under the present conditions of earthly corruption.[47]

This is clear when the verse is taken as a whole: "I tell you, brothers: *flesh and blood* cannot inherit *the kingdom of God,* nor does *the perishable* inherit *the imperishable*" (15:50). The phrase "flesh and blood" runs parallel to "the perishable," and "the kingdom of God" is paralleled by "the imperishable." So, "flesh and blood" refers to the corrupted part of bodily existence, not to bodily existence itself. Paul is not, in other words, teaching that bodily life on earth is bad and needs to be traded for life in heaven (whether that be for seven years or for eternity). Nowhere does he encourage the Corinthians to place their hope in a rapture. Instead, he wants them to anticipate the resurrection—a renewed bodily existence on the earth—which will happen at Christ's second coming (see again 15:22–23). When the trumpet blasts, says Paul, "the dead will be raised imperishable, and those who are alive at Christ's coming will be "changed" (15:52). In other words, the living and the dead will undergo physical renewal on earth. Whether a person is dead or alive when Christ returns, the "perishable body must put on the imperishable," and the "mortal body must put on immortality" (15:53). This event will be the final death of death: "When the perishable puts on the imperishable, and the mortal puts on

---

46. See, e.g., Rom 7:5, 18, 25; 8:3, 4–9, 12–13; 13:14; 1 Cor 1:26; 5:5; 7:28; 2 Cor 4:11; 5:16; 7:1; 10:2–4; Gal 3:3; 5:13, 16–17, 19, 24; 6:8, 12–13; Eph 2:3; Phil 3:3–4; Col 2:11, 13, 18, 23.

47. This seems to be different from his use of the expression in Eph 6:12. Compare Gal 1:16, where "flesh and blood" seems to carry the notion of fallibility.

immortality, then shall come to pass the saying that is written: 'Death is swallowed up in victory.' 'O death, where is your victory? O death, where is your sting?'" (15:54–55).

This means that Paul does not teach that there will be an extended time between Christ's coming and the final renewal of all things. In other words, there's no space here for a rapture *followed by* a period of tribulation *followed by* Christ's second coming. For Paul, Christ's coming is a one-and-done deal. Nothing in the context suggests a two-part event. Paul has no concept of God *removing* believers from earth; rather, he looks forward to God *renewing* humans on the earth.

ESCAPING EARTH

Everything I've said up to this point leads toward the conclusion that belief in a rapture isn't the best way to interpret the biblical evidence. Yet, at least in some circles, rapture theology persists. I think one reason for this is that *the rapture tends to nurture the idea of escapism*. For some people, the logic is that, if the world truly is going to hell in a handbasket, the only hope is to escape it—to leave earth behind. In this sense, rapture theology is rather appealing, as it allows us to leave earth as it sinks into the muck of evil. Nobody in their right mind would *not* want to escape a coming tribulation if they had the option. In the words of Hal Lindsey, "I'm getting out of here."[48] But this way of thinking has a negative effect on the way we think about this earth and how we live our lives today.

I remember a conversation I had years ago with a friend while I was in college. We were talking about all the bad stuff happening in the world. During our conversation, we discussed what the Christian response to the plight of the world should be. "It doesn't ultimately matter," he said. "It's all going to get worse anyway." His resignation was ominous. I knew exactly what he meant: Christians cannot— and perhaps should not even try to—do anything to stop the earth's

---

48. Lindsey, *Planet Earth*, 285.

downward spiral.[49] Such thinking is rooted in beliefs about the end times that are pessimistic and escapist.

Are Christians called to be escapists? Not at all. We are called to embody the kingdom of God *in this world*. In the midst of the chaos, the trials, and tribulations, we are called to be salt and light (Matt 5:13–16). We are called to be in this world, though we are not characterized by the ways of this world (John 17:14–18). We may not always realize it, but belief in the rapture creates tension with our Christian calling in this respect.

Not too long ago, I heard about an organization called After the Rapture Pet Care. This was started by believers who enlisted a cohort of non-Christians who will spring to action and rescue pets when Christians are raptured. According to the website, Christians who plan on being raptured can register their pets online to guarantee them a loving home with a non-Christian after the rapture occurs.[50] Such thinking leaves me scratching my head: apparently, we need people *not* to become Christians so they can stay behind and take care of God's creation.

This is an extreme example, to be sure. But it illustrates the mindset many Christians have today: earth, and the things of earth, do not matter to God. What matters is life in heaven, so let's outsource our calling to be caretakers of the earth during the hard times. Sadly, in some sectors of American evangelicalism, this sort of mentality is often owned and celebrated. Notice what John Hagee says:

> Other critics of the Rapture say, "The Rapture teaching is nothing but escapism. You people are trying to escape from the real world." Right now I'm living in the real world, and if I wanted to escape it, I could think of no better way than working and waiting for the coming of my Lord. But I'm thrilled that Jesus Christ is my Lord and Savior, *heaven is my home*, and that I'm not going to walk in the fires of an eternal hell. If that's escapism, so be it.[51]

---

49. N. T. Wright tells a similar story about his encounter with a group of Christians resigned to this sort of eschatological fatalism (*Surprised by Hope*, 119).

50. After the Rapture Pet Care, https://aftertherapturepetcare.com/.

51. Hagee, *Beginning of the End*, 114, emphasis added.

I think Hagee reveals the heart of the problem when he says, "heaven is my home." According to Scripture, this is *not* true. The Bible's vision for the end times is not that our final destination is heaven, but rather the renewed earth. Hagee clearly believes in the bodily resurrection.[52] But his belief in the rapture is nonetheless founded on an escapist *spiritualism*. Hagee goes on to say that the very thing he plans to escape (through the rapture) is the tribulation itself.[53]

We're tempted with the escapism of the rapture because of how awful we think a coming tribulation will be, and we don't think God would make us endure it. So at this point, it is perhaps worth asking basic questions about what the Bible says about the tribulation. Is tribulation something we are called to *endure* or to *escape*? Will there be a final, seven-year tribulation, as so many people believe?

The answers may surprise you.

---

52. See, e.g., Hagee, *Beginning of the End*, 103–4, 107.
53. See Hagee, *Beginning of the End*, 114–16.

5

IS THERE A COMING TIME OF TRIBULATION?

Many Christians believe the world is spiraling out of control and descending into unstoppable chaos. It's common to hear sermons, for example, about how the wickedness of our times far exceeds that of previous eras and how our future will get even worse than it is now. As a young evangelical, I was conditioned to think along these lines. And it was terrifying. I've since learned that this view doesn't line up well with what we know about history (the ancient world, for example, was hardly more righteous than our modern one). But such thinking nevertheless deeply influenced the way I read the Bible's end-times passages. Specifically, it caused me—and a countless number of other people—to think very narrowly about the Bible's teaching on the tribulation.

When it comes to the tribulation, the popular view goes something like this: sometime after the rapture, human history will step into the next stage of its inevitable descent into chaos.[1] After the church has been taken out of the world, the earth and its inhabitants will undergo unimaginable misery and hardship for around seven years. Some of those who missed the rapture will convert to Christ—at great risk, though. During the tribulation, the Antichrist will harness his satanic power to persecute and kill the people of God. During this

---

1. There is some debate among adherents of this view about the relationship and timing between the rapture and the tribulation. See, e.g., Hitchcock, *End*, 46–48, 233–34.

time, God's wrath will be poured out on the wicked in colossal pro-
portions.[2] One proponent of this view calls this "the darkest hour in
human history."[3]

When most evangelical Christians hear the word "tribulation,"
they tend to think of the description above—the final events. One
reason for this is the success of the Left Behind novels—the second
installment of which is titled *Tribulation Force*. Much like the rapture,
these novels shaped what an entire generation of Christians thought
about when they heard the word "tribulation."

But does the Bible teach that the world is headed toward a future
time of intense, seven-year tribulation? To answer this question, let's
take a look at some important tribulation passages.

TRIBULATION IN THE NEW TESTAMENT

First, we need to get a feel for how tribulation was understood in
the early church. In Greek, the word often translated as "tribulation" is *thlipsis*. This word occurs throughout the New Testament.
In the parable of the sower, Jesus describes those who fall away due
to "tribulation or persecution" (Matt 13:21). This assumes that "tribulation" (*thlipsis*) is a possibility for every Christian. Jesus tells his
followers, "In the world you will have tribulation. But take heart; I
have overcome the world" (John 16:33). Here Jesus seems to say that
all Christians—from the first century to when he comes again—will
experience tribulation.

In the book of Acts, Stephen retells the story of Joseph found in
Genesis and how he was sold into slavery. The word *thlipsis* is used
to describe Joseph's troubles. It's also used to recount the effects a
famine had on the land:

> And the patriarchs, jealous of Joseph, sold him into Egypt; but
> God was with him and rescued him out of all his *afflictions*

---

2. For a helpful overview of this view, see Hitchcock, *End*, 231–396, 464–66.

3. Mark Hitchcock, *101 Answers to the Most Asked Questions about the End Times* (Sisters,
OR: Multnomah, 2001), 163.

[*thlipseōn*] and gave him favor and wisdom before Pharaoh, king of Egypt, who made him ruler over Egypt and over all his household. Now there came a famine throughout all Egypt and Canaan, and *great affliction* [*thlipsis megalē*], and our fathers could find no food. (Acts 7:9–11)

Here the ESV translates *thlipsis* as "affliction," not "tribulation." This is important because most of the time, when people think of tribulation, they think of *future* final events. But in fact, this text speaks of a "great tribulation" during Joseph's era—a long time ago, in our distant past.

After Stephen was stoned, Luke reports that "a great persecution" came upon believers as a result (Acts 8:1). Luke goes on to describe this persecution as a *thlipsis* (Acts 11:19). Later, Paul and Barnabas tell believers the way into the kingdom of God is "through many tribulations [*thlipseōn*]" (Acts 14:22). Here tribulation occurs within the context of persecution from unbelievers, specifically with respect to Paul's being stoned by unbelieving Jews (see 14:19–21). This same idea is seen in Hebrews 10:33, where *thlipsis* is used to describe the persecution of Christians. Persecution is also most likely in view in Revelation 1:9, where John tells the seven churches that he is a "partner" with them "in the tribulation" (*thlipsei*).

While *thlipsis* can include the idea of persecution, it also covers the broad category of general hardships, sufferings, and adversities, like we saw in the text about Joseph. Paul may be thinking along these lines in Romans 5, where he says, "we rejoice in our sufferings [*thlipsesin*], knowing that suffering [*thlipsis*] produces endurance" (Rom 5:3). Paul echoes this same thought later on, saying, "Rejoice in hope, be patient in tribulation [*thlipsei*], be constant in prayer" (Rom 12:12). Paul doesn't seem to think Christians will escape tribulation. On the contrary, he encourages them to be patient through it.

This same idea is seen in his second letter to the church in Thessalonica. Paul applauds believers there for their faith and resolve despite their "persecutions"' and "afflictions" (2 Thess 1:4). Here "afflictions" is *thlipsesin* (tribulations). He reminds the Thessalonians that their tribulations will come to an end when Jesus returns (1:6–10). In other words, the tribulation has an expiration date.

Thlipsis can also describe the condition that results from living in a fallen world, where death, social inequalities, and various adversities threaten the well-being of the innocent. James points to this idea when he says, "Religion that is pure and undefiled before God the Father is this: to visit orphans and widows in their affliction [*thlipsis*], and to keep oneself unstained from the world" (Jas 1:27).

Together, these passages give us the big picture for how tribulation was understood by the New Testament writers. They suggest that the tribulation is not merely a future reality but a present one. They also suggest that God doesn't promise to spare Christians from tribulation; what he seems to promise is that Christians *throughout* history will go through it.[4] Perhaps years of popular prophecy teaching have made it so that we can't help but think of tribulation as a future event. But maybe this is an assumption we need to reevaluate.

All the texts examined above are fairly clear and easy to understand. But not all tribulation texts are this straightforward. Some are more complex and deserve more attention before we can decide whether they are talking about a future, end-time tribulation. One such text is Matthew 24, so I'll spend the rest of this chapter digging into what it says about tribulation.

DID JESUS TALK ABOUT A FUTURE, END-TIME TRIBULATION?

When it comes to studying the end times, and the tribulation in particular, many people make a beeline to this passage, which is often called the Olivet discourse. This is understandable because "tribulation" appears several times in this chapter, and it seems to describe the final events.

---

4. See again the last chapter on the rapture. After citing numerous NT texts that show Christians do in fact experience *thlipsis*, Brown and Keener write, "These verses confirm what Jesus and Paul said: We will have lots of *thlipsis*—tribulation!—in this world. And that leads to an obvious question: Why would we think that at the end of the age, God would spare His people from *thlipsis*? Why the final generation alone? That would seem to violate a biblical pattern, would it not?" (*Not Afraid*, 93, emphasis original).

Then they will deliver you up to *tribulation* [*thlipsin*] and put you to death, and you will be hated by all nations for my name's sake. (24:9)

For then there will be *great tribulation* [*thlipsis megalē*], such as has not been from the beginning of the world until now, no, and never will be. (24:21)

Immediately after the *tribulation* [*thlipsin*] of those days the sun will be darkened, and the moon will not give its light, and the stars will fall from heaven, and the powers of the heavens will be shaken. (24:29)

Are these texts referring to a *future*, end-time tribulation? A lot of people think so. But we shouldn't be so quick to jump to that conclusion—at least for now. After all, we've seen how "tribulation" can be used to describe *present* realities. We've also observed how the term "great tribulation" can even refer to *past* events, as in Stephen's retelling of the Joseph story. So just because we encounter these same terms in Matthew 24 doesn't necessarily mean the future is in view. It is true that the future tense is used in the above passages: "they *will* deliver you up to tribulation" and "there *will be* great tribulation" and "after the tribulation of those days the sun *will be* darkened." So, does this mean Jesus is talking about the future? Yes, but we have to ask *whose* future Jesus is talking about.

THE DISCIPLES' QUESTIONS

Prior to Jesus's talk about the tribulation, his disciples were fawning over the beauty of the temple buildings. Matthew says the "disciples came to point out to him the buildings of the temple" (Matt 24:1), and Mark records how one of them said, "Look, Teacher, what wonderful stones and what wonderful buildings!" (Mark 13:1).[5] The disciples were probably shocked at Jesus's reply: "You see all these, do you

---

5. For a description from antiquity about the temple and its beauty, see Josephus, *J.W.* 5.184–247 (esp. 5.222–223); 6.267.

not? Truly I say to you, there will not be left here one stone upon
another that will not be thrown down" (Matt 24:2). In other words,
this beautiful temple will soon be destroyed.

Later, at the Mount of Olives, the disciples ask him, "Tell us, when
will these things be, and what will be the sign of your coming and
of the end of the age?" (Matt 24:3). We need to dissect this question
carefully. In this one question, the disciples are actually asking about
two things: (1) When will "these things" occur? and (2) What is the
sign of Jesus's "coming" and "the end of the age"?[6] But what do the
disciples mean by "these things"? And how does that relate to Jesus's
coming and the end of the age? Let's take a closer look.

QUESTION 1: WHEN WILL THESE THINGS BE?

When the disciples ask this question, they are referring to Jesus's
statement about the temple's destruction: "You see all these, do
you not? Truly I say to you, there will not be left here one stone
upon another that will not be thrown down" (Matt 24:2–3). In other
words, the disciples want to know *when* the temple will be destroyed.
Jesus answers this question first, beginning in the section that immediately follows (24:4–35).[7]

QUESTION 2: WHAT WILL BE THE SIGN OF YOUR
COMING AND OF THE END OF THE AGE?

When they ask Jesus about his "coming," the disciples use the same
word we saw in the last chapter: parousia. If you remember, this
word refers to the arrival (literally, the *presencing*) of a royal dignitary to a city. By referring to Jesus's parousia, what were the disciples

---

6. R. T. France, *The Gospel of Matthew*, NICNT (Grand Rapids: Eerdmans, 2007), 890.
He says later, "The twofold focus of the question is indicated by the two interrogative markers,
'When?' and 'What sign?' as well as by the terms used, 'these things' (which in context refers
to the destruction of the temple just predicted) and 'your *parousia* and the end of the age'"
(*Matthew*, 894, emphasis original).

7. Though I disagree with him on some points, my views on the Olivet discourse are largely
indebted to France's division and understanding of the text and its relationship to the disciples'
question. See his *Matthew*, 889–94, 899. For a different view, see Osborne, *Matthew*, 868–69.

asking? They weren't thinking of a rapture, for reasons I gave in the last chapter. Neither were they thinking about Jesus's *second* coming or his return to earth in the way that we do. After all, they didn't know Jesus would leave the earth and be gone for (at least) the next two thousand years. We know this, but only because we have the advantage of having two thousand years of history behind us. It's true that Jesus had been telling his disciples he would be killed and resurrected. But they were still very much in the dark on how to comprehend this—especially in a way that would be consistent with the ministry of the Messiah.[8] In their mind, Jesus's job as Messiah was to march *visibly* into Jerusalem to be crowned as Israel's king and *publicly* free Israel from her Roman bondage. And that's the point. The disciples were asking Jesus about the signs that would accompany his *showing up*—his revealing of his messianic, kingly presence for all Israel and the world to see. They were asking about his parousia.[9]

It is interesting, too, how the disciples associated the destruction of the temple with Jesus's parousia and "the end of the age." Most likely, they assumed these events would happen all at once.[10] But Jesus subverts this idea. Even though the disciples were not expecting his parousia to be delayed—much less postponed in a *second* coming thousands of years later—this is exactly what I think Jesus teaches in this passage beginning in 24:36. Our focus below will be on the verses prior to this (24:4–35), where Jesus answers the disciples' first question about the destruction of the temple. It is in this context that Jesus refers to the *tribulation*.

---

8. For example, notice the responses of Jesus's followers when, prior to Matt 24, he speaks of his looming death and resurrection (Matt 16:21–23; 17:22–23; 20:17–19 [and 20–28]).

9. On this point, see the brief comments in Osborne, *Matthew*, 869. Though I do not track with the whole of his thought (see below) concerning the discourse, see also N. T. Wright, *Jesus and the Victory of God*, COQG (Minneapolis: Fortress, 1996), 341–42, 346. Note especially his comment: "What, after all, were the disciples waiting for? They had come to Jerusalem expecting Jesus to be enthroned as the rightful king. ... What the disciples had naturally wanted to know was, when would Jesus actually be installed as king?" (342).

10. On this, see Donald A. Hagner, *Matthew 14–28*, WBC (Dallas: Word, 1995), 687–89; see also Osborne, *Matthew*, 868–69.

THE TRIBULATION IN MATTHEW 24

In this passage, Jesus doesn't seem to be focusing on a future tribulation that will occur right before the *parousia*. Instead, he uses the word "tribulation" to describe the trials of *his* generation, not ours: "Truly, I say to you, this generation will not pass away until all these things take place" (Matt 24:34). When we stop to think about it, it does make sense why he would say this. After all, he is answering the disciples' question about *when* the temple will be destroyed ("When will these things be?"; 24:3).

It also makes sense why Jesus would talk specifically about wars, rumors of wars, and violence in this passage (24:6–7). Rome's conquest of Jerusalem and the destruction of the temple did not happen overnight. It began in AD 66 when Nero dispatched the general (and later emperor) Vespasian to push back a Jewish revolt. After Nero committed suicide, Vespasian left the siege to assume control of the empire. His son Titus took command of Roman forces, and the temple finally fell in AD 70. So naturally, the marching of imperial troops would provoke "rumors of war" in the region.[11] This would mean, obviously, that wars and rumors of war are not signs that are exclusive to the final era. They were signs of impending doom of the Jerusalem temple in the first century: "And you will hear of wars and rumors of wars. See that you are not alarmed, for this must take place, *but the end is not yet*. For nation will rise against nation, and kingdom against kingdom, and there will be famines and earthquakes in various places. All these are but *the beginning of the birth pains*" (24:6–8).

What does Jesus mean by "the end"? I think most likely Jesus is referring to the destruction of the temple—to *its* end, *its* demise. This makes sense given the context.[12] As hard as it might be for those of us

---

11. In his comment about "wars and rumors of wars," Osborne says, "The first thing that comes to mind is the revolt of AD 66–70, but in the entire period leading up to that, the Jewish people were constantly hearing such reports of devastating possibilities as well as wars between Rome and Gaul, Spain, or Britain. They were never at peace" (*Matthew*, 874).

12. See France, who thinks this is a reference to the destruction of the temple. He bases this on the fact that "end" (*telos*) here is picked up again in 24:14, which he thinks serves as a lead-in to the subsequent discussion about the destruction of the temple that follows (*Matthew*,

who have been taught that "tribulation" in the Bible always refers to our future, we need to let this passage live in the first century. This would mean that Jesus's prophecy about "the end" was fulfilled when the temple was destroyed in AD 70. This means his prophecy was *future* from the perspective of the disciples, but *past* for us.

But I want to be fair to other viewpoints here. Many people think Jesus is referring to the final events—to the end of history as we know it. So, is it *also* possible to understand "the end" as a reference to the parousia and the end of the age and hence to our future?[13] Is it possible there is another layer of meaning in addition to the first-century meaning? I think so. To see how this works, we need to inquire into the *theological* meaning behind the destruction of the temple.

THE END OF THE TEMPLE

When the temple's physical structure came to an end, its role within the life of God's people also came to an end. The temple's destruction symbolized the *end* of the Mosaic law in the sense that it was *fulfilled* and *consummated* in the ministry of Christ (see Rom 10:4). In a sense, its destruction visibly signaled the arrival of the end times. The end times, recall from the first chapter, is the final era that began with Christ's first advent and will end at his second coming. When the temple was destroyed, its sacrificial system came to an end, paving the way for the worship of God to be recentralized around the new temple of Christ, which is the church.[14]

903, 907–10). He also notes the difference in wording between 24:3 (*synteleia*) and 24:14 (*telos*; 903n31). I don't deny this view, but it is possible to see "end" as multifaceted—that is, as being embedded with layers of meaning. As I say below, with the temple's physical structure coming to an end, so will its functionality. The temple's destruction symbolizes and signals the completion of the Mosaic law in Christ and can be considered, as Osborne has said, a "harbinger" of the end times (*Matthew*, 874). So, in a sense, France is right: The "end" does refer to the temple's destruction. But we cannot miss the theological meaning behind that event (compare France's comments on the temple's destruction as "the end of the old order" on 891).

13. See, e.g., Hagner, *Matthew 14–28*, 690–92.

14. The NT teaches that Jesus's body is the temple, the place of sacrifice (John 2:18–22; note *hilastērion* in Rom 3:25; compare Lev 16:14 LXX and throughout), that the church is his body (1 Cor 12:12–31; Eph 1:22–23; 4:12; 5:29–30; Col 1:24), and that the church is therefore the new temple (1 Cor 3:16–17; 6:19). In his exchange with the Samaritan woman at the well,

In this way, the *end* of the temple signaled the *end times* (the era of the church). As the new temple, the church would carry out God's mission on the earth for many years to come. Like the first-century temple, the church will find its own end—its consummation—at the parousia of Christ at the end of the age. So, when Jesus talks about "the end," he *might* have two different, though deeply connected, meanings in mind—namely, the temple's destruction and the final consummation at the second coming.[15]

What this would mean is that, until Jesus's return, the world will carry on as normal: it will be full of chaos, wars, famines, earthquakes, and various other forms of pandemonium. These "signs" are signs of the end times, but remember, "end times" simply means the time between Jesus's first and second comings. So, these are not signs exclusive to the final few years before his return. They speak of the tribulation the church is enduring as it continues its mission as the new temple. Such tribulation will be continual and ongoing up until "the end." The mission will require sacrifice, perhaps even martyrdom. Earlier, Jesus told his followers that sacrifice—and possibly even death—awaited them (Matt 16:24). Thus, tribulation is a reality for all disciples of Jesus: "In the world you will have tribulation" (John 16:33).

THE GOSPEL AND THE END

This same idea can be seen in Matthew 24:9–14, where Jesus discusses tribulation. This passage immediately follows the one above that spoke about wars, famines, and earthquakes:

> Then they will deliver you up to tribulation [*thlipsin*] and put you to death, and you will be hated by all nations for my name's sake. And then many will fall away and betray one another and hate one another. And many false prophets will arise and

---

Jesus prophesies that worship will soon be decentralized and thus no longer exclusively associated with any one geographical location such as the temple at Jerusalem (John 4:19–24). See France, *Matthew*, 891.

15. Compare Osborne, who speaks of a "salvation-historical connection" between the destruction of the temple and the eschaton (*Matthew*, 869).

lead many astray. And because lawlessness will be increased, the love of many will grow cold. But the one who endures to the end will be saved. And this gospel of the kingdom will be proclaimed throughout the whole world as a testimony to all nations, *and then the end will come.*

This passage occurs in the same context of Jesus answering the disciples' question about when the temple will be destroyed. It truly was a season of tribulation, littered with false prophets and deceivers. The Jewish historian Josephus testifies to this fact, saying there were many "false prophets" leading people astray during the Jerusalem siege in the first century.[16] But what does Jesus mean by "the end will come" once the gospel has been preached "throughout the whole world" (Matt 24:14)? Should we take this to mean that the end of the age won't come until the gospel is taken to the whole world? Most likely, when Jesus talks about "the end," he refers not to the end of the age, but once again to the temple's destruction. When he says "the end will come" after the gospel has been preached to "the whole world," Jesus simply refers to how the gospel will spread "far outside Judea" before the temple is destroyed in AD 70.[17] Given that the context is certainly about the destruction of the temple, I think this view has a lot going for it. And, too, it makes sense of how "world" often has nonliteral meanings in Scripture.[18]

But in light of what I said earlier about dual meanings, it's also possible that another layer of meaning can be detected here. Jesus could *also* be referring to the end of the age and the worldwide proclamation of the gospel. This would make sense of how in the Great Commission, just four chapters later, Jesus connects the worldwide preaching of the gospel to the end of the age. There Jesus tells his followers to take the gospel to "all nations." As they do, he reminds them that he

---

16. See, e.g., Josephus, *J.W.* 6.285–287.

17. France, *Matthew*, 907–9.

18. For discussion and biblical references, see France, *Matthew*, 909; compare Hagner, *Matthew 14–28*, 696.

is with them "to the end of the age" (Matt 28:18–20).[19] Therefore, it's not unreasonable to think Jesus cryptically refers to the end of the age in this passage as well. In other words, even though Jesus is primarily talking about a first-century event, he *possibly* intends a dual meaning for the distant future.

What this would mean is that up until the end of the age, the world will be immersed in chaos—wars, rumors of wars, nation fighting nation, and persecution (Matt 24:6–9). The events that surround the temple's destruction ("the end") visibly signal the era of the end times—an era that will culminate at the parousia and the end of the age. Throughout this long period of history, false messiahs and false prophets will arise.

> And Jesus answered them, "See that no one leads you astray. For many will come in my name, saying, 'I am the Christ,' and they will lead many astray. ... And then many will fall away and betray one another and hate one another. And many false prophets will arise and lead many astray. And because lawlessness will be increased, the love of many will grow cold." (Matt 24:4–5, 10–12)

If Jesus intended a dual meaning in this passage, it would make sense because the events described above could be found in any era (from the first to the twenty-first century). There may be wars and rumors of wars, he says, "but the end is not yet" (24:6). These sorts of things "are but the beginning of the birth pains" (24:8). The tribulation is just the *beginning*, and Jesus teaches the tribulation will occur while the gospel goes out to all the nations. All followers of Jesus are called to "endure" until "the end" (24:13). We are to continue sharing the message of Jesus throughout the world and through all periods of history despite persecution. Once the gospel has been preached to the entire world, then the end will come (24:14). The point, once

---

19. Compare 28:20, "the end of the age" (*tēs synteleias tou aiōnos*), with Matt 24:3, "the end of the age" (*synteleias tou aiōnos*).

more, is that these tribulations are ongoing until the end. The tribulation is not, therefore, something exclusive to the final era. It's the reality of every era.

Even though it's *possible* that a dual meaning of tribulation can be detected in these passages, it doesn't negate the fact that Jesus is *primarily* talking about the destruction of the temple in the first century.

THE ABOMINATION OF DESOLATION

In the next section of Jesus's words in Matthew 24, he turns to speak about something called the "abomination of desolation." Is that about the first century, too, or is he referring to something far in the future? Here is the relevant passage, Matthew 24:15–22:

> So when you see *the abomination of desolation* spoken of by the prophet Daniel, standing in the holy place (let the reader understand), then let those who are in Judea flee to the mountains. Let the one who is on the housetop not go down to take what is in his house, and let the one who is in the field not turn back to take his cloak. And alas for women who are pregnant and for those who are nursing infants in those days! Pray that your flight may not be in winter or on a Sabbath. For then there will be *great tribulation*, such as has not been from the beginning of the world until now, no, and never will be. And if those days had not been cut short, no human being would be saved. But for the sake of the elect those days will be cut short.

We should remember that here he is continuing to answer the disciples' first question ("Tell us, *when* will these things be?," Matt 24:3).[20] Jesus doesn't give his disciples a date, but he gives them the next best thing, namely, an event known as "the abomination of desolation."

---

20. On how this begins to answer the question of 24:3, as well as how 24:15–28 relate to 24:4–14 via *oun* ("So") in 24:15, see France, *Matthew*, 910; see also John Nolland, *The Gospel of Matthew*, NIGTC (Grand Rapids: Eerdmans, 2005), 972.

And he says this will happen within *their* lifetime (24:34). But what
is the abomination of desolation?

This phrase comes from the prophecies of Daniel, which speak
about a pagan ruler who desecrates the temple (see Dan 9:27; 11:31;
12:11). Most commentators think Daniel was originally referring to
the Greek ruler Antiochus Epiphanes IV.[21] Antiochus desecrated the
temple by placing on its holy altar an idol or pagan altar to Zeus
Olympios, on which pigs were subsequently sacrificed.[22] Jewish literature from the time period also describes this act as "an abomination of
desolation" (1 Maccabees 1:54, my translation; compare 2 Maccabees
6:2–5). This event took place in 167 BC. So when Jesus quotes Daniel's
"abomination of desolation," he is recalling Antiochus's desecration of
the temple that occurred some two centuries before.

Obviously, Jesus can't be talking about Antiochus. He had long
been dead when Jesus was born. Jesus is using the story of Antiochus's
desecration of the temple as a *type* of another desecration that is
coming. This is why Matthew inserts the comment, "let the reader
understand" (Matt 24:15; see Mark 13:14). Matthew knew Jesus was
pointing to something else. But who, or what, was Jesus referring to?

This has something to do with the Roman destruction of the
temple. In Luke's account of Jesus's speech, this becomes clear: "But
when you see Jerusalem surrounded by armies, then know that its
desolation has come near" (Luke 21:20). What does this refer to?
Admittedly, the details are murky. Some scholars point to Josephus's
comment that, when the temple was taken over, the soldiers made
pagan sacrifices on the temple grounds (*J.W.* 6.316).[23] Whatever the

---

21. See, e.g., André Lacocque, *The Book of Daniel*, trans. David Pellauer (Atlanta: John
Knox, 1979), 197–99; Daniel L. Smith-Christopher, *Daniel*, NIB (Nashville: Abingdon, 1996),
128; France, *Matthew*, 911; Nolland, *Matthew*, 970; Wright, *Jesus and the Victory of God*, 349–51.

22. Lacocque, *Daniel*, 198, 229; Smith-Christopher, *Daniel*, 128; Josephus, *Ant.* 12.253. There
is, however, some ambiguity regarding the historical details of the events that took place here.
On this, see David A. deSilva, *Introducing the Apocrypha: Message, Context, and Significance*, 2nd
ed. (Grand Rapids: Baker Academic, 2018), 272; Robert Alter, *The Hebrew Bible: The Writings:
A Translation with Commentary* (New York: Norton, 2019), 3:788n28.

23. See, e.g., Nolland, *Matthew*, 971, although see the critique in France, *Matthew*, 912–13;
compare Hagner, *Matthew 14–28*, 701. See also the comments on Mark 13:14–16 in Wright, *Jesus*

specifics, the "abomination" refers generally to events having to do with the Roman siege, the invasion, and destruction of the temple—a desecration if there ever was one.

When all of this begins to take place, Jesus warns his followers to leave the area immediately (Matt 24:16–20). Regarding the brutality of the coming war, Jesus says: "For then there will be *great tribulation* [*thlipsis megalē*], such as has not been from the beginning of the world until now, no, and never will be. And if those days had not been cut short, no human being would be saved. But for the sake of the elect those days will be cut short" (Matt 24:21–22). Notice how Jesus calls this the "great tribulation." He draws once again from the prophecy of Daniel: "And there shall be a time of trouble, such as never has been since there was a nation till that time" (Dan 12:1b). In the Greek version of Daniel, "a time of trouble" is *kairos thlipseōs*, literally, "a time of tribulation" (Dan 12:1b [Theodotion]). Here Jesus repurposes the prophecy to describe what life will be like during the Roman siege of Jerusalem and the subsequent destruction of the temple.

Some prophecy teachers think this is a reference to an end-time tribulation, pointing out that Jesus says this will be the worst event in history.[24] But Jesus could be employing hyperbole, a rhetorical device he used often in his teaching ministry.[25] Again, the context is clearly the destruction of the temple in AD 70, so we need to anchor the language of tribulation there. His point is to answer the disciples' question about the destruction of the temple. A futurist interpretation is possible, but only insofar as it is relevant to *that* original question.

With that said, let's think a bit more about how a futurist interpretation of Matthew 24 might work. To do this, we will need to look at the way prophecy functions in the Bible.

---

and the Victory of God, 352–53, 360.

24. See, e.g., the comments in LaHaye, *Revelation*, 132–33.

25. See, e.g., Luke 14:26. On hyperbole in Matt 24:21, see Hagner, *Matthew 14–28*, 702. Osborne thinks this language points to how Jerusalem's destruction foreshadows events of the final era (*Matthew*, 886).

THE LOGIC OF PROPHECY

I argued above that Jesus used Daniel's phrase "the abomination of desolation" to refer to the destruction of the temple by the Romans— an event, he said, that would happen during his generation's time (Matt 24:34). In fact, it did happen. We might say Jesus repurposed Daniel's original prophecy for his own time. Whereas Daniel originally spoke about a Greek empire desecrating the temple, Jesus applies Daniel's words to another beastly empire of his own day, the Roman Empire.

But here's where things get interesting. When we dig a little deeper into Daniel's prophecy, we see that he too repurposed an even older prophecy spoken by Jeremiah. Originally, Jeremiah had prophesied that the exile would last for seventy years, but Daniel grew concerned that something wasn't quite right and revisited the prophecy (Dan 9:1–2; see also Jer 25:11–12; 29:10).[26] So the angel Gabriel was dispatched to reveal a new layer of meaning regarding Jeremiah's prophecy. He tells Daniel the original prophecy of "seventy years" of exile actually means *seventy years of seven periods* (= *years*). In other words, 490 years (Dan 9:24). The point is that Jeremiah's *past* prophecy is reunderstood by Daniel in such a way that it can now speak about hardships created by Antiochus much later, in the second century BC.

On the surface, this rereading of Jeremiah's prophecy might seem arbitrary, but it's not. In the Torah, the covenant stipulated that, should Israel continue in rebellion against God, they would be punished "sevenfold" (Lev 26:18, 21, 28). This allows for Jeremiah's original seventy years to become Daniel's seventy times seven. So, Daniel's

---

26. Smith-Christopher says, "Jeremiah's seventy years ... was probably not intended to be a precise number in the first place, and may simply have meant an entire lifetime, so that Jeremiah was telling the exiles that *they*, undoubtedly, would never see Palestine again, even if their children would. But because the exile did not end, and a new David was not on the throne, and also because the foreign nations remained in power, later Jewish scholars, mystics, and seers returned to contemplate the possible meanings of Jeremiah's promised end of exile. And this is the question that Daniel is pondering" (*Daniel*, 121, emphasis original).

interpretation can be seen as different from and yet still consistent with Jeremiah's original prophecy.

The way biblical prophecy often works is that the original word can be extended into future events and realities. This is true even if the original prophecy leaves little to no hint of a futurist application. Sometimes past events and activities can be repeated in the future. This repetition is often described as a fulfillment of the original prophecy.

An example of this is Hosea 11, where God, through the voice of the prophet, sings of his love for Israel as he recalls his rescue of his people from Egypt at the exodus: "When Israel was a child, I loved him, and out of Egypt I called my son" (Hos 11:1). Here Israel is depicted as God's beloved "son." When we arrive at the New Testament, we discover this text is applied to Jesus when he and Mary and Joseph return from Egypt after having sought refuge there from Herod. Matthew 2:14–15 says, "And he rose and took the child and his mother by night and departed to Egypt and remained there until the death of Herod. *This was to fulfill what the Lord had spoken by the prophet, 'Out of Egypt I called my son.'*"

Matthew takes a prophecy that originally spoke about the nation of Israel and repurposes it as a reference to Jesus. Jesus's leaving Egypt is interpreted as a new exodus event. For Matthew, Jesus embodies Israel's story. Yet, nothing in the original context of Hosea would suggest this interpretation. Hosea was not even predicting the future. In fact, he was recalling the past. Yet Matthew speaks of this as a prophecy that was *fulfilled* in Jesus's return from Egypt.

This captures the logic of biblical prophecy. As I said in a previous chapter, prophecy cannot be reduced to a *prediction* and *fulfillment* scheme. It is perhaps more beneficial to speak about prophecy in terms of a *drama* that is *performed* or as an *act* that exists to be *reenacted*.[27] In other words, biblical prophecy can have on some level

---

27. My views on this are inspired by the hermeneutics of Hans-Georg Gadamer, particularly with respect to his notion of "play" and "drama." See my *Paul and the Meaning of Scripture.*

multiple layers of meaning. This is how Hosea's prophecy worked for Matthew. It's how Jeremiah's prophecy worked for Daniel. It's also how Daniel's prophecy worked for Jesus. Jeremiah made a prophecy that was later repurposed by Daniel. Jesus then takes Daniel's repurposed prophecy and repurposes it once more.

All of this could shed light on whether "tribulation" language in Matthew 24 refers exclusively to the first century *or* to the distant future *or* on some level both. Jesus's warnings about the abomination of desolation and the tribulation refer to events that happened in the first century. I think this is clear. But given how biblical prophecy works, it's also *possible* these events could be reenacted in the future.

Let's be cautious, though. Just because it's possible that the tribulation of Matthew 24 will be repeated in the future does not mean we can be certain about all the possible details. That's why those who think the abomination of desolation will be reenacted by a future Antichrist need to tread carefully. While this is possible and maybe even likely (if we assume Jesus has a dual meaning), we need to admit the ambiguity of the details. For example, one should not take references to "wars and rumors of wars" or "famines" or "earthquakes" or "tribulation" or "great tribulation" out of their original context in Matthew 24 in order to speculate about particular events in the distant future. We can only *speculate*, which is a risky enterprise for fallible interpreters.

The only way we can be sure a prophecy is going to be reenacted is when it ends up being reenacted. If Matthew 24:1–35 speaks of future events, we can only know the details when we reread that text *after* the events occur (like Matthew does with Hosea *after* Jesus is ascended). Until then, we must admit some prophecies are shrouded in mystery. In the meantime, we should never interpret texts in ways that contradict Scripture. Daniel's prophecy did not contradict Jeremiah's original prophecy. Likewise, Jesus's prophecy did not contradict Daniel's. At the end of the day, we have to admit the obvious when it comes to end-times prophecy: there's a lot we simply can't know.

IS THE WORLD HEADED TOWARD
A FUTURE TRIBULATION?

But here's what we can know. When Jesus does explicitly talk about the final events—specifically, about his second coming—he does it in such a way that he creates some distance between it and the specific "great tribulation" that he has been speaking about. In Matthew 24:21–28, for example, Jesus says that during the destruction of the temple, there will be messianic pretenders who will arise. This, he says, will create confusion about his return. But Jesus tells his disciples not to worry about this because when he actually does return, everyone will know it. It will be *public, visible,* and *unmistakable.* It will catch every eye, like lightning across the sky: "For as the lightning comes from the east and shines as far as the west, so will be the coming [*parousia*] of the Son of Man" (24:27).[28]

Given that it has been nearly two thousand years since the temple was destroyed *and* given the obvious fact that Jesus has yet to return, this is significant. Why? Because it shows the "great tribulation" of Matthew 24 is not something that happens *right before* the final events—contrary to modern prophecy teaching.

And, strictly speaking, once the temple was destroyed in AD 70, it's only *that* specific tribulation that has ended. It doesn't mean tribulation itself is over. The context is all about the disciples' question regarding the destruction of the temple—something that happened in our past, a long time ago. Jesus uses the word "tribulation" to describe *that* event.

This means that "tribulation" in Matthew 24 is not used explicitly to refer to events in our future. Jesus himself, after all, says these events will be fulfilled in his generation's time (24:34). *Even if* Jesus

---

28. On this point, I'm indebted to France, who says, "This verse is a sort of 'aside' which draws a sharp distinction between the events during the siege and the still future *parousia.* ... [Jesus] is thus setting the *parousia* and the end of the age decisively apart from the coming destruction of the temple. ... So the mention of the *parousia* in this context is intended precisely to distinguish it from the events currently being considered" (*Matthew,* 917–18, emphasis original).

cryptically refers to our future (which, again, I think is possible), that still does not mean "tribulation" is *exclusively* about a future event. Why not? Because his warning about tribulation must *also* have been relevant for his own generation.

We can now end our look at the tribulation in Matthew 24 with this very important conclusion: *the tribulation is that long period of time that stretches from Jesus's era to the final events.* Matthew 24 doesn't suggest that the world is headed toward a future tribulation. It suggests we're already in it.

TRIBULATION NOW?

Some might question the idea that the church is currently in the tribulation. Many of us live in the ease and comforts of Western culture. But it would be a mistake—not to mention arrogant—to identify the church with Western Christianity. The Christian family is larger, indeed a great deal larger, than the church in the West. Just because American Christians, for example, are not being killed for their faith does not mean the church is not under threat elsewhere in the world.

Christians in Southeast Asia, for example, are threatened, imprisoned, and killed often for their faith. Christians in Africa, too, are often afflicted with persecution and various forms of tribulation. Christians who live in relative ease should identify with and carry the burdens of their brothers and sisters in other parts of the world such that *they* would never be blinded to the fact that the church is being persecuted. In the future, our roles might be reversed. There may come a time when American Christians are killed routinely for their faith while Asian Christians live in comfort.

But some would object. How can "tribulation" refer to the destruction of the temple in AD 70 when Jesus says that "immediately" after the tribulation is over, everyone will see him "coming on the clouds of heaven with power and great glory" (Matt 24:29–30)? In other words, if Matthew 24 is all about the destruction of the temple, then why didn't Jesus come back, riding on the clouds for all to see? Doesn't this mean that the interpretation I'm proposing is wrong and that the tribulation of Matthew 24 must refer exclusively to a *future* tribulation?

I don't think so. After all, why should we assume that Jesus's "coming on the clouds of heaven" refers to his second coming? That might sound like a silly question, but it's one that needs to be asked. In fact, when we dig deeper into the context of this mysterious phrase, we discover that it actually has more to do with Jesus *going to heaven from earth* than *coming to earth from heaven.*

6

HOW CAN WE KNOW WHEN JESUS WILL RETURN?

The most important event on the prophetic calendar is the bodily return of Jesus. All Christians look forward to the day when Jesus will return to resurrect and restore the saints to the earth. This will be the moment of great renewal, a time when this world—riddled with eras of brokenness and tribulation—will finally be repaired and recreated. At his coming, Jesus will bring comfort to all God's people (John 14:1-3). It will be the moment when the cosmos finally experiences the peace that was purchased through Christ's sacrificial death. All things will be healed, and everything will be made new (Col 1:20; Rev 21:1-5). When Jesus returns, he will bring the freedom for which we long and were made.

But when will this happen? Are there future events that will serve as definite signs of Christ's imminent return? Some people think so. They look to Matthew 24, for example, where Jesus says people will see him "coming on the clouds," which will take place "immediately after the tribulation" (24:29-30). Many prophecy teachers think this refers to the second coming of Christ after a future end-time tribulation.[1] In many ways, it's understandable why people would think this. Elsewhere in Scripture, for instance, Jesus's second coming is described as an event that takes place "in the clouds" (1 Thess 4:17). So when Jesus talks about his "coming on the clouds" in Matthew 24, that same idea is easily read into it.

---

1. See, e.g., LaHaye, *Revelation*, 103-5, 302.

But is this view correct? If it is, then it would mean the tribulation mentioned in that passage (24:29) doesn't primarily—or at all—have to do with the destruction of the temple in the first century (something I argued for in the last chapter). After all, Christ obviously didn't return *immediately* after the destruction of the temple in AD 70. And too, if Jesus was talking about his second coming in this passage, then it would mean that we *can* know when Jesus will return—namely, right after the future tribulation. Is it true, then, that a future end-time tribulation will be the clue we need to know that Jesus's return is right around the corner?

Not exactly. We need to look carefully at what the passage actually says: "Immediately after the tribulation of those days" (Matt 24:29). Notice that Jesus is speaking only about the tribulation "of those days." This comment occurs after his discussion about the abomination of desolation and the destruction of the temple, which he previously described as a "great tribulation" (Matt 24:21). So when Jesus says "immediately after the tribulation" in 24:29, *that* specific event is what Jesus means by "tribulation." Again, the evidence suggests that his entire discussion is about the destruction of the temple (see the last chapter). Strictly speaking, once that event was over, the tribulation "of those days" was in fact over. This is consistent with the view that the tribulation is ongoing through history. So by describing it as a "tribulation *of those days*," Jesus refers to just one cycle of the ongoing tribulation that exists between his resurrection and his return. So far, so good.

But what about Jesus's statement about "coming on the clouds"? Doesn't this refer to Jesus's second coming? While some well-respected biblical scholars would disagree, I don't think this is a reference to Jesus's second coming, or parousia.[2] To see why, we need to look closely at the words Jesus uses: "*The Son of Man coming on the clouds of heaven with power and great glory.*" This comes from Daniel 7:13. The word

---

2. See Wright, *Jesus and the Victory of God*, 361 (commenting on the Markan parallel; Mark 13:24–31). However, the view that Matt 24:30 does refer to the parousia is held by some well-respected biblical scholars, such as Donald Hagner (see *Matthew 14–28*, 713–14) and Grant Osborne (*Matthew*, 894–95).

used for "coming" is not the word *parousia*, which is routinely used throughout this text to refer to Jesus's return. The word Jesus uses instead is *erchomai*, which is taken from the Greek version of Daniel. As we will see, the "coming of the Son of Man" here doesn't have anything to do with a person coming *from* heaven. Instead, it's a Jewish expression for the enthronement of God's anointed ruler *in* heaven.

THE CONTEXT OF DANIEL

In Daniel 7:1–8, the prophet sees four beasts come up out of the sea. These represent four kingdoms of the world: Babylonian, Median, Persian, and Greek. The vision then moves to a spectacular scene of God (called "the Ancient of Days"), who is sitting on a heavenly throne and presiding in judgment. The kingdoms of the world are subsequently judged and destroyed (Dan 7:9–12). At this point, Daniel sees the Son of Man coming to the Ancient of Days to receive a universal and everlasting kingdom:

> I saw in the night visions,
>
>> and behold, with the clouds of heaven
>>> there came one like a son of man,
>> and he came to the Ancient of Days
>>> and was presented before him.
>> And to him was given dominion
>>> and glory and a kingdom,
>> that all peoples, nations, and languages
>>> should serve him;
>> his dominion is an everlasting dominion,
>>> which shall not pass away,
>> and his kingdom one
>>> that shall not be destroyed. (Dan 7:13–14)

This is an important passage for two reasons. First, the context is about the Son of Man inheriting the nations of the world. It is about his enthronement as king. Because he stands before the Ancient of

Days—that is, before God himself—he is publicly enthroned before the sight of the heavenly court (and by extension, the inhabitants of the earthly realm). Second, this text has nothing to do with the Son of Man coming to the earth. In fact, the word used for "coming" (*erchomenon*) can actually be translated as "going." The idea has more to do with the Son of Man going *to the heavenly realm*, where God's throne and heavenly court reside.[3]

So, when Jesus talks about his "coming" in Matthew 24:30, he is not talking about a return to earth. He is talking about his vindication and victory over the nations in the *heavenly* realm. The "sign of the Son of Man" he mentions appears in heaven, not on the earth (Matt 24:30). This is the scene of action. As we will see below, the idea is divine warfare in the spiritual realm. That's why Jesus talks about the sun and moon going dark, the stars falling from heaven, and the powers of the heavens being shaken (Matt 24:29). Here Jesus draws from the rich symbolism of Old Testament passages, specifically from Isaiah 13:10 and 34:4. We need to take a closer look at these passages so we can get the full scope of what Jesus is talking about.

In Isaiah 34:4, we read: "All the *host of heaven* shall rot away, and the skies roll up like a scroll. All their *host shall fall*, as leaves fall from the vine, like leaves falling from the fig tree." Here the falling heavenly "host" (*tsava*) refers to spiritual beings.[4] In the Greek Old Testament, which is the source for Matthew's text, the Hebrew word *tsava* ("host") is translated as *ta astra* ("the stars"). In the Bible, cosmic bodies such as stars were often associated with spiritual beings.[5] That's why I think, when Jesus uses cosmic language here, he refers to

---

3. On the idea that the Son of Man moves from earth to heaven (and not heaven to earth), see Lacocque, *Daniel*, 137; see also France, *Matthew*, 396, 923; Wright, *Jesus and the Victory of God*, 361.

4. John Goldingay, *Isaiah*, NIBC (Peabody, MA: Hendrickson, 2001), 194.

5. See Michael S. Heiser, *Unseen Realm: Recovering the Supernatural Worldview of the Bible* (Bellingham, WA: Lexham Press, 2015), 23–24, esp. n. 3. He points to texts such as Job 38:7 and Isa 14:13–14 as well as several others. See also the discussion in Caird, *Revelation*, 89–90; Werner Foerster, "Ἀστήρ, Ἄστρον," *TDNT* 1:503–5; Nolland, *Matthew*, 982–83.

spiritual warfare in the spiritual realm.[6] This would make sense, especially in light of his comment that "the powers of the heavens will be shaken" (Matt 24:29), which seems to be a clear reference to spiritual beings (compare Eph 1:21; 6:12). The spiritual warfare theme is very important for understanding the biblical idea of tribulation (more on this in a moment).

But this does not mean Jesus's coming is *merely* an otherworldly event, as if it has no bearing on earthly realities. Jesus's vindication here is in fact very earthly, public, and for all to see: "all the tribes of the earth will mourn" (Matt 24:30). To better understand what Jesus means by this, along with his talk of "coming on the clouds" and tribulation, we need to look at a scene that takes place two chapters later, in Matthew 26.

JESUS AS THE TEMPLE OF GOD

In Matthew 26:57–68, Jesus finds himself arrested and standing before Caiaphas, the Jewish high priest. The entire scene is a joke. The religious leaders can't find anything of which to legitimately accuse him. Out of desperation, they lob false accusations against him. At one point, two "witnesses" come forward and accuse Jesus of threatening to destroy and reconstruct the temple in three days' time (Matt 26:60–61). They are referring to the time when Jesus angrily ran all the corrupt money changers out of the temple. When asked what sort of sign he could present to show he had a right to disrupt the temple business, Jesus gave a simple answer: "Destroy this temple, and in three days I will raise it up" (John 2:19). The Jewish officials

---

6. This is not to say that Jesus is referring exclusively to spiritual warfare. There is more, but certainly not less, going on with Jesus's use of cosmic language. R. T. France, for example, is correct to highlight the political and historical context of Jesus's discussion here. He rightly says that Jesus is operating here in the same vein as the OT prophets, who used "language about cosmic collapse ... to symbolize God's acts of judgment within history, with the emphasis on catastrophic political reversals. When Jesus borrows Isaiah's imagery, it is reasonable to understand it in a similar sense. If such language was appropriate to describe the end of Babylon or Edom under the judgment of God, why should it not equally describe God's judgment on Jerusalem's temple and the power structure which it symbolized?" (*Matthew*, 922).

are perplexed. How can one man possibly perform such a feat? This is where John adds a brief explanatory comment into the text: "But he was speaking about the temple of his body. When therefore he was raised from the dead, his disciples remembered that he had said this, and they believed the Scripture and the word that Jesus had spoken" (John 2:21–22). For Jesus, there was a close relationship between his own body and the temple of Jerusalem. When he spoke about one, he could refer to the other.

When Caiaphas hears this accusation against Jesus, he demands an answer. But Jesus remains silent (Matt 26:62–63). In response, Caiaphas exclaims: "I adjure you by the living God, tell us if you are the Christ, the Son of God" (26:63). This is where Jesus replies with a quotation from Daniel 7:13: "Jesus said to him, 'You have said so. But I tell you, *from now on* you will see *the Son of Man seated at the right hand of Power* and *coming on the clouds of heaven*'" (Matt 26:64).

Notice that Jesus doesn't quote the passage from Daniel as a reference to the far distant future; he quotes it as a reference to his *present* moment. He tells Caiaphas that "from now on" he and his entourage will behold the reality of Daniel's Son of Man.[7] In other words, his "coming" is happening as he speaks with Caiaphas. This means Jesus could not be talking about his second coming, to his parousia at the end of time. He must be referring to something else.

One clue this is correct is how the language of "coming on the clouds of heaven" is joined to the previous phrase, "seated at the right hand of Power," which alludes to Psalm 110:1. Both phrases point to Jesus's enthronement and authority over the cosmos—privileges reserved only for a divine ruler. Caiaphas understands this. That's why he immediately tears his clothes and accuses Jesus of "blasphemy" and hence being worthy of death (Matt 26:65–66).

Notice also that Jesus doesn't say, "You will see the Son of Man seated at the right hand of Power *and then* coming on the clouds

---

7. The "you" in both "But I tell you" and "you will see" in 26:64 is plural in Greek (*hymin* and *opsesthe*, respectively).

of heaven." Jesus doesn't speak of sequential events but concurrent events. The image seems like an oxymoron: How can someone be *seated* and *coming* at the same time? But once we see how ancient Near Eastern people understood what it meant for a deity to ride the clouds, the image will make better sense.

RIDING THE CLOUDS

As Mike Heiser, a respected Old Testament scholar, notes, in the ancient world the concept of riding on the clouds was used to describe the activity of a deity—most notably the pagan god Baal. Old Testament writers reappropriated this language and applied it to Yahweh in order to depict him as the supreme deity.[8] Heiser points to texts such as the following:

> There is none like God, O Jeshurun,
>> who *rides through the heavens* to your help,
>> through the skies in his majesty. (Deut 33:26)

> O kingdoms of the earth, sing to God;
>> sing praises to the Lord ...
> *to him who rides in the heavens, the ancient heavens;*
>> behold, he sends out his voice, his mighty voice.
>> (Ps 68:32–33)

> Bless the LORD, O my soul!
>> O LORD my God, you are very great!
> You are clothed with splendor and majesty,
>> covering yourself with light as with a garment,
>> stretching out the heavens like a tent.
> He lays the beams of his chambers on the waters;
> *he makes the clouds his chariot;*
>> *he rides on the wings of the wind;*

---

8. Heiser, *Unseen Realm*, 251–52. He says, "The literary tactic made a theological statement. The effect was to 'displace' or snub Baal and hold up Yahweh as the deity who legitimately rode through the heavens surveying and governing the world" (252). Compare Smith-Christopher, *Daniel*, 104.

> he makes his messengers winds,
>> his ministers a flaming fire. (Ps 104:1–4)

An oracle concerning Egypt.
Behold, the Lord is riding on a swift cloud
>> and comes to Egypt;
> and the idols of Egypt will tremble at his presence,
>> and the heart of the Egyptians will melt within them.
>>> (Isa 19:1)

Caiaphas knew the image of the Son of Man coming on the clouds implied the action of God. He wasn't picturing Jesus's second coming or anything of the sort. Caiaphas was too immersed in the stories of the Old Testament to think like that. Instead, he pictured exactly what Daniel envisioned years before—the enthronement of the true king.

Jesus tells Caiaphas that from the point of their conversation onward, he will be enthroned and inherit the nations, just like Daniel prophesied. What did Jesus mean by this? On the one hand, Jesus's prophetic ministry would have been vindicated when the temple was physically destroyed a few decades later (AD 70). When Jesus prophesied the temple would fall, he was laughed at and mocked (Matt 27:40–44; Mark 15:29–30; John 2:20). But those living during the tumultuous years of Rome's destruction of the temple would have remembered the prophecy of Jesus. After the temple fell, his identity as a prophet—indeed, as the Son of Man—would have been vindicated. He would have been publicly shown to be right all along.

I think Jesus also meant something else. When Jesus tells Caiaphas that "from now on" he will see the Son of Man "coming on the clouds," he is referring to his suffering, death, resurrection, and ascension. In other words, Caiaphas (and others) will see Jesus's enthronement *through* these events. Through these acts, Jesus will assume rule over the nations. This makes sense of other passages that say Jesus conquered the spiritual forces of evil through his death. For example, Colossians says Jesus's crucifixion (and resurrection) "disarmed the rulers and authorities and put them to open shame, by triumphing over them" (Col 2:15). In 1 Corinthians, we learn that, had the forces of evil known their killing the Son of Man would secure their destruction, they wouldn't have done it (1 Cor 2:8). Paul says Jesus's resurrection revealed his true identity and vindicated his divine sonship (Rom 1:4; 1 Tim 3:16). According to many other texts, Jesus's ascension to the Father's right-hand side inaugurated his rule over the earth (Ps 110:1; Eph 1:20–23; Heb 1:3–4, 13; 10:12–13; 12:2). The New Testament also teaches that Jesus's coming to the Father actually initiated a war in the heavenly realm that in turn led to a war being started on the earth—all of which eventually culminates in the ultimate demise of Satan and his forces of darkness (we will return to this idea in a moment).

It's important to understand that Jesus viewed his body as the place of sacrifice—that is, as the temple. It would be destroyed but then raised back up (John 2:21). The ultimate abomination of desolation was the murder of the Son of God. But the resurrection and ascension of his temple-body vindicated who he said he was all along: the Son of Man, the King of kings, the ruler of the nations—the nations from which he will "gather" a people (Matt 24:31).[9] Caiphas would have a front-row seat to all of these events. This is what Jesus meant by "coming on the clouds." It was a reference to the destruction of the temple—both of them, in fact: the Jerusalem temple and his body. Through both the temple's demise and his crucifixion, Jesus would assume rule over the nations—he would *ride the clouds*.

We need to keep all of this in mind when we read Jesus's words in Matthew 24. His coming on the clouds is not about his second coming but about his vindication as a prophet who foretold the destruction of the temple (24:30). It makes sense, then, why Jesus would say his coming would occur "immediately after the tribulation of those days" (24:29). Jesus's vindication culminates in the destruction of the temple.

---

9. On the role the phrase "gather his elect" plays in Jesus's vindication, see France, *Matthew*, 926. With France, I take this verse to refer to the evangelization of the nations (927–28).

WAR IN HEAVEN

What happened when Jesus came *riding on the clouds* as the Son of
Man, *coming* to God to inherit the nations? In short, a war broke out
in heaven. More specifically, Revelation 12 suggests the tribulation
began at the ascension of Christ.[10] In this chapter, which is full of symbols and otherworldly images, we read about "a woman clothed with
the sun" (Rev 12:1). The moon lies under her feet, and she is crowned
with twelve stars. She is also pregnant and about to give birth. A ferocious character is then introduced: a seven-headed dragon with ten
horns. The dragon, having pulled down to earth a third of the stars,
takes his place in front of the woman, eager to consume the child
once he's born. This child is destined to "rule all the nations with a
rod of iron," and after he is born, he is taken up to heaven, "caught up
to God and to his throne" (12:5). We then read how the woman flees
into the wilderness, where God takes care of her for 1,260 days (12:6).

Once the son has been taken to the throne, a war breaks out in the
heavenly realm. When Jesus arrives, the dragon fights Michael and
his army but quickly loses. The dragon and his evil forces are then
exiled from heaven, cast down to the earth (12:7–9). Then a voice,
belonging perhaps to an angel, describes Christ's coming to the throne
of God as the coming of "salvation" and "power" and kingly rule and
"authority" (12:10). The angel can say this because of what his coming
has brought about: the casting down to earth of the dragon—Satan,
the diabolical accuser of God's people. He has been defeated because
Christ has done what Daniel prophesied long ago.

Even though Jesus has taken up his throne and defeated the dragon in
the heavenly realm, things on earth are about to heat up. The angel warns
that the dragon comes with "great wrath" (12:12). The dragon rages after
the woman, seeking to kill her. But she is supernaturally protected. She
is "given the two wings of the great eagle," which allows her to fly to the
wilderness, where God protects her "for a time, and times, and half a time"
(12:14). The dragon then attempts to drown her in a flood, but the earth

---

10. Keener, *Revelation*, 34.

protects her. Having failed yet again, the dragon spirals into a diabolical mania, making war "on the rest of her offspring, on those who keep the commandments of God and hold to the testimony of Jesus" (12:17). The "rest of her offspring" is a reference to Christians of every era.[11]

Because the Son of Man has *come to* the Ancient of Days, the dragon lost his access to heaven and consequently his ability to accuse God's people. It is in this sense that the saints "have conquered him by the blood of the Lamb and by the word of their testimony" (12:11). This is why Paul can say, "There is therefore now no condemnation for those who are in Christ Jesus" (Rom 8:1). By assuming the heavenly throne, Christ destroyed the devil's power. But Christ's ascension and victory do not guarantee the church's comfort. If anything, it has put the enemy in a frenzied obsession to bring tribulation to the world and to the church in particular (Rev 12:12, 17).

This is further evidence that the tribulation began two thousand years ago at Christ's ascension and will last until Jesus returns.[12] From the time Christ ascended and put the dragon in a rage (Rev 12) to the day the dragon is destroyed at Christ's second coming (20:7–10), the church—along with the world—will experience trials and tribulations. This is exactly what Revelation 12 refers to when it uses symbolic numbers and phrases such as "1,260 days" and "time, and times, and half a time":

> and the woman fled into the wilderness, where she has a place prepared by God, in which she is to be nourished for *1,260 days.* (Rev 12:6)[13]

> But the woman was given the two wings of the great eagle so that she might fly from the serpent into the wilderness, to the place where she is to be nourished for *a time, and times, and half a time.* (Rev 12:14)

---

11. See the discussion as well as response to potential objections in Keener, *Revelation,* 324–25.

12. Keener, *Revelation,* 34–35, 318–20, 327, 333.

13. Daniel mentions 1,290 and 1,335 days (Dan 12:11–12). On this, see Keener, *Revelation,* 318n30; John Goldingay, *Daniel,* rev. ed., WBC (Grand Rapids: Zondervan, 2019), 551–52.

These numbers come out to three and a half years if 1,260 days is based on a 360-day year calendar and if "time" (in the phrase "a time, and times, and half a time") is the equivalent of a year.[14] These are also allusions to Daniel 7:25, which in its Old Testament context referred to Antiochus's brutal reign: "He shall speak words against the Most High, and shall wear out the saints of the Most High, and shall think to change the times and the law; and they shall be given into his hand for *a time, times, and half a time.*" The phrase "time, times, and half a time" could be for Daniel a specific reference to a period of Antiochus's persecution of Judea, which can be calculated to around three and a half years. But according to one scholar, precise calculations probably miss the point. It's simply a way of saying Antiochus's reign is limited and will be abruptly cut short—it's half of the symbolically loaded number seven.[15]

Revelation probably means something similar. The dragon will have a reign of terror, but this season of tribulation will not last forever. God has limited it. This is why the text says "his time is short" (Rev 12:12). Thus, the number is perhaps not necessarily a literal three and a half years of tribulation, but a symbolic way of referring to the limited time between the first and second coming of Christ.[16] It's simply saying, "It won't last forever. The dragon will come to an end." If the number seven implies fullness, then by speaking of three and a half years, John is simply saying the tribulation has an expiration date. Until then, Christians are called to faithfully represent Christ. By "the word of their testimony" and the "blood of the Lamb," we conquer the enemy (Rev 12:11).

Interestingly, this same period of time is applied to the first Beast of Revelation 13. After the dragon determines to wage war against God's people, he summons a Beast from the sea through whom he

---

14. Keener, *Revelation*, 318; see also 319, 322.

15. See the argument in Goldingay, *Daniel*, 381; compare Lacocque, *Daniel*, 153–54.

16. Keener says, "The 1260 days may refer to the period between the first and second comings of Jesus, characterizing the entire church age as a period of tribulation in some sense" (*Revelation*, 35; see also 319, 322). See also Brown and Keener, *Not Afraid*, 164–66.

can bring carnage. This Beast is said to reign for "forty-two months" (Rev 13:5). As I said in a previous chapter, the Beast represents on some level Nero and his Roman Empire. The number is still symbolic in the way I described above. It represents the entire church age, with Nero's reign serving as an ongoing symbol of the dragon's turbulent fury against the church throughout history. The church's tribulation has been ongoing through the centuries, and it will continue until Christ returns. So, the answer to the question I posed at the beginning of the chapter (How can we know when Jesus will return?) is clear: we can know when Jesus will return when the tribulation ends. But that raises an interesting point, doesn't it? After all, we can't know for certain when Jesus will return because we simply don't know how long the tribulation will last. By definition, the "tribulation" is that long span of time between Christ's first and second coming.

But won't we be able to know Jesus's coming is imminent when the tribulation gets more severe? It is possible (and I suspect likely) that there will be a peculiar season of persecution and tribulation right before Christ returns.[17] This would actually make a lot of sense. Think about it: Daniel's prophecy about the "abomination of desolation" of the Jewish temple originally referred to how the Greeks profaned the temple nearly two hundred years before Christ was born. But Jesus repurposed Daniel's prophecy to predict that the Roman Empire would destroy the temple in AD 70. So *perhaps* the abomination of desolation will once again be reenacted in our future. We don't know whether this will happen, as Jesus nowhere says it will. It's purely speculative. Even if this will happen, however, it doesn't give us permission to begin constructing elaborate timelines of tribulation events and start making predictions about Christ's coming. That would be unwarranted and even irresponsible.

---

17. I'm indebted to Keener for this idea. He thinks an "intensification of suffering" at the end is possible, but even if so, it "is probably not the primary point in Revelation" (*Revelation*, 35). See also Brown and Kenner, *Not Afraid*, 161–63, 165 (esp. 162).

Even though I believe we are currently living in the tribulation, we can't know the timing of when various events will occur. Even if the current tribulation were to unfold in a series of severe events, how could we know that those will be the final tribulation events? We can't. After all, things might get even worse later, or they might cycle back around to something better—only perhaps to get worse once again. We simply don't know how long the tribulation will last or how (or when) it will ebb and flow back and forth between bad and severe events. We don't know the number of ups and downs that will occur before the second coming of Christ. That's why we can't know exactly *when* Jesus will return, either.

But doesn't Revelation give us a play-by-play of particular events that will take place sometime in the future, right before the return of Christ? Many prophecy teachers believe that when the plagues of Revelation and the four horsemen of the apocalypse arrive, these will be sure signs and clear signals that Christ's return is right around the corner. Is this correct?

DEMONIC ARMIES OF THE APOCALYPSE

In Revelation 6–18, we read about three cycles of wrath that afflict the earth and its inhabitants. Each of these cycles is divided up into seven installments: seven seals (Rev 6:1–17; 8:1–5), seven trumpets (8:6–9:21; 11:15–19), and seven bowls (16:1–21). Some think these chapters, and the three cycles in particular, describe a future seven-year tribulation, with each cycle occurring consecutively, one right after the other.[18] Others think the three cycles "parallel one another," that is, they speak of the same event.[19] I suspect something like this is correct.

---

18. See, e.g., LaHaye, *Revelation*, 100, 132, 137–39, 141. It is worth noting that, while LaHaye thinks the three sets of judgments are consecutive, he doesn't think Revelation as a whole should be read as if each consecutive chapter speaks of consecutive events (see, e.g., 136, 138, 178, 196).

19. Keener, *Revelation*, 34. Keener says this is the "dominant view" (34); compare Witherington, *Revelation*, 129–31. For an overview of the debate, see deSilva, *Discovering Revelation*, 106–8.

One reason I opt for this view is that at the end of each series of judgments (seals, trumpets, and bowls), there is a finality that suggests the world's judgment has come to an end. Craig Keener is right to observe, "The sort of events closing the seals, trumpets, and bowls cannot repeat unless the world as we know it can come to an end several times (these three references plus 19:11–21)!"[20] It is interesting that the seventh trumpet seems to announce the end of wrath and the consummation of the kingdom of God (Rev 11:15–19). Yet, the seven bowls have yet to be poured out. How can this be? The problem is solved if we read these texts as speaking about the same events in three different ways throughout Revelation.

Do these cycles of judgment refer just to the future? According to LaHaye, the first two cycles (seals, trumpets) take place during the first half of a future seven-year tribulation, with the last cycle (bowls) occurring at the last half.[21] But this interpretation is more specific than these texts call for. After all, there is a lot in these texts that could apply to the present era.[22] When you take time to read through these judgments, you will notice rather quickly that there's not a lot of specificity about them. One scholar says, "Most of these judgments are so general they could represent events in many ages of human history."[23] He's correct.

For example, let's look at the first four seals of Revelation 6:1–8, which collectively have become known as the four horsemen of the apocalypse. The first horseman is given the power to "conquer," and the second is allowed "to take peace from the earth" (6:2–4). The third carries a scale of weights and is associated with economic injustice and inflation (6:5–6). The fourth horseman is granted authority

---

20. Keener, *Revelation*, 34. See also 398 for his caution against reading each individual judgment within a series as consecutive and sequential (note this occurs in his comment on the bowls of Rev 16).

21. LaHaye, *Revelation*, 138–39. For LaHaye, the tribulation doesn't kick off until the Antichrist shows up and strikes a seven-year covenant with Israel. That event won't happen, he says, until sometime after the rapture (see 139–40).

22. Keener, *Revelation*, 34–35, 199–200.

23. Witherington, *Revelation*, 131.

to kill one-fourth of the earth's population by the "sword," "famine," "pestilence," and "wild beasts" (6:7–8).

The first three horsemen could easily describe any point of history. The fourth could, too.[24] The point with the fourth horseman is that humans who continue in their willful rebellion will be handed over to the evils of this age and be judged. The mention of one-fourth of the population is simply to say the judgment is not comprehensive or complete at this point. In Revelation, numbers typically have a symbolic function, not a literal one. So the point here seems to be that it is within God's loving nature to hold back the full force of his judgment as he waits for people to repent (see 2 Pet 3:1–10).[25] This same idea could apply to some of the other judgments in Revelation as well. Clearly, the judgment is not complete with the fourth horseman because the opening of the next seal says so, as the martyred saints ask God how long until it's over—implying, of course, that it is *not* over yet (Rev 6:9–11). The sixth and seventh seals do seem to describe the future—but only in the sense of a final judgment and the consummation of all things (6:12–17; 8:1–5).[26]

The cycles of judgments are filled with such highly symbolic language that literal interpretations would only lead to confusion, not clarity. In the third trumpet, for example, a "great star" is said to fall from heaven and into one-third of the earth's freshwater, polluting it in the process and causing many people to die (8:10). The star in question cannot be a literal star. If a literal star fell from outer space onto the earth, much more than one-third of earth's freshwater would be

---

24. This would include, of course, the first-century churches of Asia. The first horse, for example, might have evoked images of the army of the Parthians, the frightening enemy of the Roman Empire (Witherington, *Revelation*, 133). Keener is right to say, "Revelation uses this image merely to underscore the point of hostile invaders, not to predict a specifically Parthian invasion. The point is that Roman rule will someday collapse—not to yield an eternal rule by Parthia, but ultimately by God (11:15–19)" (*Revelation*, 202). See also deSilva, *Discovering Revelation*, 109–10.

25. Compare Keener, *Revelation*, 272–73; Witherington, *Revelation*, 130, 149.

26. Compare the sixth and seventh trumpets (Rev 9:13–21; 11:15–19) and bowls (16:12–21). See Keener, *Revelation*, 34, 220–22, 253–54.

destroyed. LaHaye thinks this is a reference to a meteorite.[27] Perhaps this is what we are to visualize. But as we saw above, "stars" in the Bible often mean spiritual beings, and on some level that seems to be the case here, too. This makes sense because just a few verses later, when the fifth trumpet is blown, a spiritual being is called a "star."[28] The fourth trumpet evokes similar astronomical language to speak of spiritual realities: "The fourth angel blew his trumpet, and a third of the sun was struck, and a third of the moon, and a third of the stars, so that a third of their light might be darkened, and a third of the day might be kept from shining, and likewise a third of the night" (8:12).

We encountered this sort of apocalyptic language already, and the symbolism here points us in the same direction, namely, to a spiritual shakeup in the heavenly realm. A literal interpretation would miss this point. As I said above, overly literal (or wooden) interpretations of apocalyptic texts often produce misunderstanding. It's unclear how a person would literally interpret the above passage, anyway. Should we think that one-third of the surface of the sun, moon, and stars literally goes dark *or* that earth loses one-third of a period of daylight and night light or both? Such questions miss the point.

Another point of this passage may be to show what happens to creation when it chooses to divorce itself from its Creator. Without God, creation falls apart and self-destructs. In the Genesis creation story, the heavenly lights (sun, moon, and stars) are given by God to the earth as *good* gifts (Gen 1:14–19). The creation story itself is a tale of how God takes the watery and dark *chaos* of Genesis 1:2 and lovingly reshapes it into *cosmos* (order). But then sin enters the world, distorting the beauty of God's good creation. Revelation narrates this tragedy by recording the consequences that sin brings: The *cosmos* devolves

---

27. LaHaye, *Revelation*, 167.

28. "And the fifth angel blew his trumpet, and I saw a star fallen from heaven to earth, and he was given the key to the shaft of the bottomless pit. He opened the shaft of the bottomless pit" (Rev 9:1–2a). On this being in particular and the verse in general, see the helpful comments from Witherington, *Revelation*, 150. LaHaye thinks the star in this verse is an "angel" (LaHaye, *Revelation*, 169).

into *chaos.* Apart from God, creation becomes undone. That's why we see the earth experiencing destruction and the heavenly lights falling into dysfunction—even to the point of harming the earth (the opposite of what they were intended to do in Genesis). Notice carefully how Revelation tells that story: in the fourth seal, *one-fourth* of the earth experiences death, famine, and pestilence (Rev 6:8). This is intensified in the fourth trumpet, when *one-third* of the sun, moon, and stars lose their light, thus blanketing the earth with darkness (8:12). This bottlenecks at the fourth bowl, when *the entire* sun is allowed to "scorch" the earth (16:8). The creation is no longer working in harmony; it's at war with itself. The point can't be missed: without God's grace, the created order will slowly—but inevitably—fall into chaos.[29]

If we think Jewishly (as the author of Revelation would surely want us to), then we must interpret these passages apocalyptically—and hence not ignore the highly symbolic and theological story they are telling. Some prophecy teachers want to interpret these texts literally and not symbolically. But those who are committed to interpreting the Bible as the authors intended ought to interpret Revelation apocalyptically—given that is what Revelation *literally* is, namely, an apocalyptic text.

I believe these seals, trumpets, and bowls speak mostly about present realities. But they also speak of future realities—this is especially true for the sixth and seventh installments of each series.[30] How, then, do we understand the sixth bowl, which tells of demons who inspire rulers of the earth to launch a great battle at a place called Armageddon (Rev 16:12–16)? Or what about a similar passage in Revelation 9:13–21, where the sixth trumpet is discussed? Here we read about sinister "angels" who lead an army of two hundred million troops that ride on mutant horses with tails like heads of snakes.

---

29. On the points highlighted here, see my article "Monkeypox and the Plagues of Revelation: Is There a Connection?" *Word by Word,* October 7, 2022, https://www.logos.com/grow/hall-monkeypox-revelation.

30. See again Keener, *Revelation,* 34.

Each mutant horse is depicted as having a head like a lion's, with fire, smoke, and sulfur spilling from its mouth.

Do these passages describe a future end-time event, and should we take these images as exact representations of what the demon horde will look like? Probably not. Again, these are intended to be taken *symbolically*, which is why we can't be too dogmatic about the details. Symbolic language allows the author to communicate spiritual realities that would otherwise evade normal language. This doesn't mean we ought to take demonic activity as any less real. Elsewhere, for example, Jesus is depicted as having eyes "like a flame of fire," and he even has a "sharp sword" coming out of his mouth (Rev 19:12, 15). To say that Jesus will *literally* have a sword coming out of his mouth would miss the point being communicated—that his word is effective and powerful. This symbolic portrait of Jesus evokes a richness that straightforward descriptive prose could not.

Regarding the Armageddon passage (the sixth bowl), we probably shouldn't think of this as a battle that takes place at one geographical location on earth. For starters, the Greek word for Armageddon is *harmagedōn*, which some scholars think refers to the Hebrew words for "Mount Megiddo" (*har* means "mountain" in Hebrew). In the Old Testament, Megiddo is the site of a battle where God and his heavenly host defeat Israel's enemies (Judg 5:19–20). But as scholars often point out, Megiddo is actually a city, not a mountain. So why would Revelation call it a mountain? Most likely, it's because Isaiah 14:13 mentions a "mount of assembly," which is the place where God and his divine council meet. It's also the site of Satan's revolt against God. Why is this important? The words "mount of assembly" in Hebrew are *har mo'ed*, with the backwards apostrophe representing a *g* sound, giving us the pronunciation *har-moged*. Some scholars think this (and not Megiddo) is what Revelation means by *har-magedōn*. But it's possible Revelation draws on both ideas. With the word "Armageddon," Revelation is able to capture two different Old Testament portraits (Megiddo and the Mount of Assembly) in order to symbolize and describe *both* intense spiritual rebellion *and*

God's ultimate victory over it. In doing so, the word probably has more symbolic than geographical meaning.[31]

When it comes to the sixth trumpet, this vision most likely communicated to its original readers some sort of demonic army.[32] But this doesn't necessarily mean the text is presenting an exact image of what the event will—if indeed it is future—look like.[33] Again, it's written in symbolic language. But also, spiritual beings are quite capable of doing their work behind the veil, so to speak—that is, without physically looking demonic (consider, for example, Jesus's rebuke of Peter in Matt 16:21–23).

Demonic activity can manifest itself in a plethora of ways—through people, societal structures, unjust institutions, to name a few. Of course, it can also be overt and visible. Why, then, should we assume the sixth trumpet depicts an actual picture of demonic activity? Any speculation about the image this text evokes should be tempered by focusing on the point of the passage, which is embedded in its rich imagery. A careful reading of the passage shows the point is to encourage a steady faithfulness and devotion to Jesus and not sell oneself out to demonic allegiances that traumatize us—such as the Roman Empire for John's first-century audience.[34]

Once we understand the symbolic nature of these judgments, it opens the door to fuller expressions of meaning. Specifically, when the need to look for *exclusively* future applications is less urgent, we will be in a much better position to focus on the true meaning of, say, the four horsemen of the apocalypse that bring havoc on the earth. In other words, we can focus our attention on concerns such as war, economic injustices, and the fact that people around the world are

---

31. My view on Armageddon outlined above is somewhat eclectic, drawing from scholars such as Heiser (*Unseen Realm*, 83–91, 358–75), Beale (*Revelation*, 838–41), and Caird (*Revelation*, 205–7).

32. On this, see deSilva, *Discovering Revelation*, 117.

33. Keener suggests interpreters focus on the vision's overall "message" and not so much "the details of the image" that is depicted in that vision itself (*Revelation*, 275).

34. DeSilva, *Discovering Revelation*, 117–18.

currently dying of diseases that could be cured if only they had access to modern medicine. Sadly, when we don't look for the symbolic meaning of Revelation's images, we can become blinded to the fact that these sinister spiritual forces have already arrived. They've been here for a long time, in fact. Perhaps the enemy's war tactic all along has been to get us to think so much about the future that we are blind to his nefarious activity in the present.

CALLED TO BE FAITHFUL IN A TIME OF WAR

When Christ ascended and cast Satan down to the earth, Satan became furious. He seeks to take his rage out on the inhabitants of earth. And as Christians, we need to be faithful to Christ and guard against the devil's schemes. Peter writes, "Be sober-minded; be watchful. Your adversary the devil prowls around like a roaring lion, seeking someone to devour" (1 Pet 5:8). In Paul's words, this is war: "For though we walk in the flesh, we are not waging war according to the flesh. For the weapons of our warfare are not of the flesh but have divine power to destroy strongholds" (2 Cor 10:3–4). Our battle is not against other people, but against dark forces of the spiritual realm: "For we do not wrestle against flesh and blood, but against the rulers, against the authorities, against the cosmic powers over this present darkness, against the spiritual forces of evil in the heavenly places" (Eph 6:12).

Satan is already a defeated enemy. Jesus conquered him at the cross. We participate in that victory over evil by our union with Christ and our faithful witness to him (Rev 12:11). Jesus, the Son of Man—the cloud rider himself—has been enthroned, and he alone is the king of all nations and empires. Jesus has all authority in the *spiritual* and *earthly* realm. That's why he has sent us to reclaim the nations for himself. Every time we advance the gospel across the earth, we are taking ground from the enemy. Satan was banished to earth, but Jesus has sent us to reclaim it, leaving the enemy without refuge.

And Jesus came and said to them, "All authority in heaven and
on earth has been given to me. Go therefore and make disciples
of all nations, baptizing them in the name of the Father and
of the Son and of the Holy Spirit, teaching them to observe
all that I have commanded you. And behold, I am with you
always, to the end of the age." (Matt 28:18–20)

Our mission is costly and dangerous. Like John, we are participants
in the tribulation, and we are called to exhibit "patient endurance"
(Rev 1:9). We also have the promise that Christ, and his peace, is
with us through it all (Matt 28:20; John 16:33). We cling to the hope
that, one day, Jesus *will* return to fix everything. Right now, creation is
undone, but when Jesus returns, it will be redone. The created order,
which slides back toward a state of primeval chaos (Gen 1:2), will be
recreated and renewed. Or as my four-year-old says, "When God
turns earth into heaven, there won't be any more bad guys." Indeed,
paradise lost will one day be paradise restored.

THERE'S MORE TO COME

To say the tribulation is already present is not to say it also isn't future.
Every present moment of church history will experience tribulation—
right up to the end of the age. That's why every Christian throughout history rightly anticipated and longed for the return of Jesus. It
is very possible, and I think likely, that the groaning and tribulation
the earth currently experiences will bottleneck into something very
challenging at the end. Perhaps the demonic army of the sixth trumpet symbolically envisions this very thing. Spiritual warfare will be a
reality then just as it is now. All the same, we should not point to any
of our trials and think those are specific signs that Christ will necessarily return in our lifetime. There's no way we can know that. The
fact is we should be ready *at all times* for the return of Christ. When
he does return, he will put an end to our trials.

He will also bring an end to someone the Bible calls the Antichrist.
But as we will see in the next chapter, the Bible teaches there are many

antichrists throughout history. It also teaches that there will be a *final* Antichrist. But there's a lot of confusion about this nefarious figure. There are so many preconceived ideas about the Antichrist that, to some confessing Christians at least, I fear the future Antichrist (like many other antichrists throughout history) might not look like anything sinister at all.

Indeed, he may even look appealing.

7

WHAT CAN WE KNOW ABOUT THE ANTICHRIST?

He's the world's final nemesis, the symbol of the apocalypse itself. Most conversations on eschatology lead back to this mysterious figure. Many Christians wonder whether the Antichrist is already alive with boots on the ground. Some speculate that he's still a young man, being groomed this very moment to become the world's foremost geopolitical strategist. Some think he's already on the political scene but currently undercover. Many think he's going to show up soon, though. At just the right moment (soon after the rapture), he will jump on the world's stage and enact his diabolical plan of world domination.

In a book published some twenty-five years ago, John Hagee surmises, "This so-called man of peace, this son of Satan, this false messiah, the Antichrist, is probably alive right now and may even know his predestined demonic assignment. And though we may not know who the Antichrist *is*, we certainly know in great detail what the Antichrist will *do*."[1] This quote captures the mentality of many Christians today. Such speculation is common especially among American evangelicals, who have for a long time been drawn to the suspicion that the final Antichrist has already arrived.

Many have speculated about his nationality, his ethnicity, and even his views on economics. Some have said that the Antichrist is going

---

1. Hagee, *Beginning of the End*, 135, emphasis original.

to be a Muslim.[2] Tim LaHaye once mused that he will be a "Roman-Grecian Jew," though keeping his Jewish lineage hidden. He even goes on to say the Antichrist will be a socialist.[3] John Hagee thinks the Antichrist might even be a Nobel Peace Prize winner.[4] Not too long ago, a rumor was floating around that Revelation teaches the Antichrist will be a forty-something year-old man.[5]

All of this is interesting in light of what the Bible actually says about the Antichrist. As a matter of fact, Revelation says nothing about the age of the Antichrist. Technically, it says nothing at all about the Antichrist. If you search for the word in Revelation, it doesn't even turn up (though it does turn up elsewhere in the New Testament, as we'll see). That people can speak with such certainty about these things can appear baffling. When we pay attention to what the Bible does (and does not) say about the Antichrist, we discover there's actually not a lot of detail given. There's a lot of general information, sure. But the specifics are hard to come by. (Spoiler alert: nothing in the Bible says the Antichrist will be a socialist or a Muslim.)

But as students of Scripture, our first priority is to follow the biblical evidence. We need to ask ourselves: What does the Bible actually say?

THREE TERMS, THREE TEXTS

There are three terms often associated with the final nemesis. The first, of course, is "the Antichrist." This is the most popular description. It's one most people recognize. The second is "the Beast," which

---

2. Daniel Burke, "How the 'Islamic Antichrist' Reflects Our Era's Anxieties," Religion News Service, February 6, 2013, https://religionnews.com/2013/02/06/how-the-antichrist-reflects-an-eras-anxities.

3. LaHaye, *Revelation*, 209, 211.

4. Hagee, *Beginning of the End*, 118.

5. According to Amy Hollyfield, there was a rumor (proliferated through an email chain) going around in 2008 that erroneously claimed "The Book of Revelations" taught the Antichrist would be a forty-year-old Muslim man. The email made the not-so-subtle suggestion that then-Senator Barack Obama could possibly be the Antichrist. See Amy Hollyfield, "According to the Book of Revelations the Anti-Christ ... Will Be a Man, in His 40s, of MUSLIM Descent ... Is It OBAMA??," PolitiFact, April 2, 2008, https://www.politifact.com/factchecks/2008/apr/02/chain-email/complete-distortion-of-the-bible.

comes from Revelation. This is well-known, too. It's often taken to be synonymous with the Antichrist. Finally, the third term is perhaps the least familiar: "the man of lawlessness." Each of these terms can be found in Scripture. However, none of them can be found together in the same place. Many people think all three of these people are synonymous, that they speak about the same person. There are similarities between them, as some have recognized.[6]

Like we saw in a previous chapter, the Beast of Revelation was associated with the Roman Empire, specifically Nero and Domitian. I have no problem giving Nero and Domitian—and the empire as an institution—the title "Antichrist." They were certainly *anti*-Christian. A lot of people view the Beast as an end-time figure and thus as *the* Antichrist. This would make sense. Like I said earlier, even though the Beast certainly has to do with the first century, it goes beyond that. I'll say more about this later.

I think a strong case could be made that the man of lawlessness is the Antichrist the Bible talks about. Revelation doesn't talk about him explicitly, but Paul does. The information Paul provides is interesting, though I'm not sure we can glean too many details about this figure. Paul speaks rather vaguely about him. But there is enough evidence that we can walk away knowing something significant.

In the pages that follow, we will look at each of these three figures. As we dive into the relevant texts, it will be important to take a step back from any assumptions you have about the Antichrist. You can always pick them back up later. But in the meantime, hold them tentatively. Let Scripture have its voice as you hold your assumptions up to its scrutiny.

THE ANTICHRIST

The word "antichrist" comes from the Greek *antichristos* and appears just five times in the New Testament: four times in 1 John (2:18, 22; 4:3) and once in 2 John (2 John 7). Out of these five, only one is a

---

6. See, e.g., the brief discussion in Wright and Bird, *New Testament and Its World,* 798 (and 428).

reference to the final Antichrist. The others use the word only to
describe antichristian types of people. Notice the following passage,
where the first three references occur.

> Children, it is the last hour, and as you have heard that *anti-
> christ* is coming, so now many *antichrists* have come. Therefore
> we know that it is the last hour. They went out from us, but
> they were not of us; for if they had been of us, they would have
> continued with us. But they went out, that it might become
> plain that they all are not of us. ... Who is the liar but he who
> denies that Jesus is the Christ? This is the *antichrist*, he who
> denies the Father and the Son. No one who denies the Son has
> the Father. Whoever confesses the Son has the Father also. ... I
> write these things to you about those who are trying to deceive
> you. (1 John 2:18–19, 22–23, 26)

The first occurrence seems to be a reference to the final Antichrist.
Notice how John distinguishes this Antichrist from the "many antichrists" (2:18). In doing so, John seems to have a specific individual
in mind, namely, a *final* nemesis.[7]

What's interesting, however, is the lack of information John provides. In the context of the passage, no details are given. He mentions
the Antichrist only in passing. This is sort of frustrating to those
of us who want to know more. It makes sense, though, why John
doesn't say more than he does. It was never his intention to write
an exposé on the final events. John's primary concern, instead, was
about deception running through the church (2:26). Apparently, false
teaching had become a problem, with some denying that Jesus was
the Messiah (2:22). Some in the church had even abandoned their
faith altogether (2:19).

Later on, John tells the church to "not believe every spirit" and to
"test the spirits." The reason, he says, is that "false prophets" have arisen
(4:1). If a spirit or self-proclaimed prophet failed to acknowledge that

---

7. On 2:18, Hoekema reaches the same conclusion (see *Bible and the Future*, 158).

Jesus had come in human form, then they failed the test. John warns, "Every spirit that does not confess Jesus is not from God. This is the spirit of the antichrist, which you heard was coming and now is in the world already" (1 John 4:3). Like I said, John isn't that interested in the final events. He is, however, interested in the end times, which is technically a different, though related, matter.[8] Notice how he describes the times in which he lives: "Children, it is the last hour" (2:18) This can be translated "last hour" or "end hour" or perhaps "end time." For John, the end times has already begun—and it's full of antichrists.

In 2 John, there is one more antichrist reference. John writes to someone he calls "the elect lady." He addresses her "children" as well (2 John 1). It's hard to know who exactly this lady was. Perhaps she served as a pastor or minister of some sort. Her "children" seem to be the congregation. Whatever her role, she is clearly a leader in charge of the discipleship of believers who are under her care. John encourages her and the church to continue walking in love toward one another and follow God's commandments (2 John 5–6). He warns her about "many deceivers" who don't believe "the coming of Jesus in the flesh" (2 John 7).

This doesn't seem to refer to nonbelievers outside the church, but rather to those who were infiltrating the church. Apparently, these people denied the physical nature of Jesus's person. In the early years of Christianity, there was a false teaching known as docetism, which taught that Christ looked human, but he actually wasn't. These false teachers seem to think along these lines. John says someone who teaches these sorts of things "is the deceiver and the antichrist" (2 John 7; see also 1 John 4:1–3).[9] Those are strong words. But it makes sense of what they were doing. They were teaching that Christ himself was deceptive: He looked physical, but he wasn't. In doing so, they were creating a false Christ in the place of the true Christ. Their work truly was *deceptive* and *anti-Christ*.

---

8. See again ch. 1.

9. For a discussion about these false teachers, especially in regard to the question of docetism, see Wright and Bird, *New Testament in its World*, 790–95, 799–800, 803; see also Hoekema, *Bible and the Future*, 157–58.

WHAT JOHN SAYS (AND DOESN'T SAY)

Out of the five references to "antichrist," only one has to do with the final Antichrist, and this is only mentioned in passing. As a result, there are not a lot of specifics we can learn from just these passages. But taken together, we can glean several bits of information that will help us craft a *basic* understanding about the concept of antichrist.

THERE ARE MANY ANTICHRISTS

John says many antichrists were present during his day (1 John 2:18; 22; 4:3; 2 John 7). This is because he, like us today, was living in "the last hour" (1 John 2:18). This is consistent with Jesus's warning to his disciples that they should be aware of "false christs" and "false prophets" (Matt 24:24). Throughout history, we have seen antichrist figures and antichristian movements. One thinks, for example, of Adolf Hitler and Joseph Stalin, both of whom were monsters of a recent generation. Today, Christians are persecuted—sometimes tortured and killed—in various parts of the world just because they are Christians. As we will see, though, "antichrist" cannot be relegated to just mass murderers and physically violent persecutors. The passages above show that "antichrist" mainly has to do with false teaching.

ANTICHRISTS ARE ASSOCIATED WITH FALSE TEACHING AND DECEPTION

Most of us only think of Antichrist as a geopolitical leader of the final events. But here, he is nowhere associated with politics. John speaks of antichrists only in the sense of false teaching and deception. In his era, antichrists sought to lead people astray from the true faith. In doing so, these antichrists act as "forerunners of the final antichrist."[10] This leads us to our next observation.

THERE IS A FUTURE ANTICHRIST

The one verse that speaks of a future Antichrist is 1 John 2:18. Strictly speaking, John never says this Antichrist will come at the end of the age.

---

10. Hoekema, *Bible and the Future*, 158.

All he says is that "antichrist is coming" and moves on. How frustrating! But I get it. John's primary concerns didn't include mapping a timeline of the future, but addressing present issues afflicting the church of his era. All we know from this verse is that Antichrist was coming sometime in *his* future. Does this mean John was referring to a final Antichrist? I think there is plenty of evidence to suggest he was.[11]

You have probably noticed that every time I refer to the *final* Antichrist in this verse, I have capitalized the word—"Antichrist." This is not capitalized in the translation that I have been using in this book (ESV). But I have chosen to do this because I think this figure does refer to a final nemesis—the final, end-time Antichrist. Part of my reasoning is that John seems to set this person apart from all the others: "you have heard that antichrist is coming, so now many antichrists have come" (2:18). I suspect, then, that all the other references to antichrists living in John's day, as well as the ones that continue to pop up in the future, have to do with antichrists in general. The other reason is how I understand Paul's statement about a final nemesis he calls "the man of lawlessness" (2 Thess 2:3). There are key similarities between that passage and John's discussion here that make me think they are speaking about the same person.[12] I will talk more about these later.

A FUTURE ANTICHRIST WAS WIDELY DISCUSSED IN THE FIRST CENTURY

I get this idea from how John qualifies some of his statements about Antichrist. Notice how he says, for example, that "it is the last hour, *and as you have heard that antichrist is coming,* so now many antichrists have come" (1 John 2:18). Apparently, the early church was *already*

---

11. See again Hoekema, who says, "We may grant that the thought of a single future antichrist is not very prominent in John's epistles; his emphasis falls mostly on antichrists and antichristian thinking which is already present in his day. Yet it would not be correct to say that John had no room in his thinking for a future personal antichrist, since he still looks for an antichrist who is coming" (*Bible and the Future,* 158).

12. On John having in mind a future and final Antichrist, see the helpful discussion in Hoekema, *Bible and the Future,* 158.

aware that some mysterious figure would show up. This means the
teaching that the Antichrist would come in the future did not originate
with John's letter. Perhaps John had previously taught them about the
Antichrist. Or maybe someone else did. Either way, the teaching about
an antichrist-type person predated John's letter because Paul mentions
"the man of lawlessness" in his second letter to Thessalonica, which
was written before 1 John.[13] In fact, Paul himself says he taught the
Thessalonians about this before he penned the letter (2 Thess 2:3–5).
So, I think we can say with some confidence that the teaching about
a future nemesis was well-known in the early church.[14]

These are some conclusions we can draw from John's discussion. There's no mention that the future Antichrist will be a political
figure. There's no discussion about his ethnicity or his nationality. This
doesn't mean Antichrist couldn't be a political figure. I'm just saying
we can't know this from these texts.

THE "ANTI" IN ANTICHRIST

Before we move on, I want to say a few things about the word "antichrist." In Greek, the word is *antichristos*, a combination of two Greek
words, *anti* and *christos*. You're probably familiar with both. The word
christos is where we get "Christ," and it means "anointed one"—the
Greek equivalent of the Hebrew Messiah. The other word, *anti*, has
a different meaning from what you may expect. In English we use it
often to convey the idea of "to stand against" or "to be contrary to
something or someone." For example, we speak about anti-anxiety
medication or an antidemocratic regime. But in Greek, *anti* is a preposition that can have a different meaning from this. The word *anti*
often conveys the idea of taking the place of something or someone

---

13. According to Wright and Bird, 1 John might have been composed sometime in the latter
part of the first century—though no later than the AD 80s or 90s. An earlier date than this is
certainly within the realm of possibilities, too (*New Testament in Its World*, 789–90). Moreover,
they muse that 2 Thessalonians was most likely written around AD 50 (pp. 416–19). On John
likely having been familiar with Paul's teaching on the man of lawlessness in 2 Thessalonians,
see Hoekema, *Bible and the Future*, 158.

14. So Bruce, *1 & 2 Thessalonians*, 179; see also Hoekema, *Bible and the Future*, 158.

else or exchanging one thing or person for another.[15] Look at the following examples:

> But when he heard that Archelaus was reigning over Judea *in place of* [*anti*] his father Herod, he was afraid to go there, and being warned in a dream he withdrew to the district of Galilee. (Matt 2:22)

> You have heard that it was said, "An eye *for* [*anti*] an eye and a tooth *for* [*anti*] a tooth." (Matt 5:38)

> What father among you, if his son asks for a fish, will *instead* [*anti*] of a fish give him a serpent? (Luke 11:11)

> See to it ... that no one is sexually immoral or unholy like Esau, who sold his birthright *for* [*anti*] a single meal. (Heb 12:16)

> *Instead* [*anti*] you ought to say, "If the Lord wills, we will live and do this or that." (Jas 4:15)

In my opinion, this is part of the idea behind John's *antichristos*. He's not merely saying this person will *overtly* stand against Christ as an outsider of the church, but rather *deceptively* redefine Christ inside the church.[16] When we take a look at Paul's description of the man of lawlessness, we will see this same idea. If I am correct, then many Christians—evangelicals in particular—have for years been looking in the wrong direction. The Antichrist threat probably doesn't come from outside our walls but within them. I fear his spirit has won over a lot of gullible believers.

THE MAN OF LAWLESSNESS

In 2 Thessalonians 2:1–12, Paul talks about an enigmatic figure who shows up sometime before Christ's second coming. He calls him "the

---

15. See Daniel B. Wallace, *Greek Grammar beyond the Basics: An Exegetical Syntax of the New Testament* (Grand Rapids: Zondervan, 1996), 364–68.

16. Working with both definitions of *anti*, Hoekema rightly describes *antichristos* as "a substitute Christ or a rival Christ" and "an *opponent* of Christ" (*Bible and the Future*, 157, emphasis original). Compare his comments about the man of lawlessness on 160.

man of lawlessness" and "the son of destruction" (2:3).[17] Paul provides much more information about this person than John does about the Antichrist. Like I said above, I think it's reasonable to think these two people are the same. The similarities between the two seem to point in that direction. First, we need to observe everything Paul says about this shadowy individual.

Paul raises the subject in the context of correcting misconceptions about the second coming of Christ. Some in the church had been led to believe that Christ had already returned. The text suggests that someone misled them through false teaching or forged a letter to deceive the church into thinking Paul and his ministry team were themselves teaching this.[18] This understandably led to much fear among the believers (2 Thess 2:1–2).[19] Paul responds, saying such teaching is false (2:3). Christ has not yet returned. They can know this for certain because the Lord's return cannot happen until after a certain event. He says,

> Let no one deceive you in any way. For that day will not come, unless the rebellion comes first, and the man of lawlessness is revealed, the son of destruction, who opposes and exalts himself against every so-called god or object of worship, so that he takes his seat in the temple of God, proclaiming himself to be God. Do you not remember that when I was still with you I told you these things? (2 Thess 2:3–5)

This passage is loaded with information, and we need to carefully dissect each piece to learn what exactly Paul is saying.

---

17. Gene L. Green has observed that "the son of destruction" was also a title given to Judas (John 17:12), who betrayed Jesus. See Green, *The Letters to the Thessalonians*, PNTC (Grand Rapids: Eerdmans, 2002), 308.

18. On the situation, see the discussion in Green, *Letters to the Thessalonians*, 303–5.

19. On this second "coming" (2 Thess 2:1) being the same event described in 1 Thess 4:13–18, see Bruce, *1 & 2 Thessalonians*, 163. See again ch. 5, where we examined 1 Thess 4:13–18 and found it *not* to be a reference to the so-called rapture.

PAUL IS TALKING ABOUT THE DISTANT FUTURE

This passage appears to speak about the distant future. Most likely, Paul anticipated the man of lawlessness would be revealed sometime nearer his own time—perhaps even in his own generation. He might not have thought he was talking about *far distant* events of the future. From our perspective, though, the man of lawlessness is far removed from Paul's era. There's no way we can know when exactly he will show up. That said, Paul does drop a clue about an event that will happen around the time of the revealing of the man of lawlessness. He calls it "the rebellion" (2 Thess 2:3).

THE REBELLION

What does Paul mean by "the rebellion"? To be honest, I'm not sure about the details. Paul doesn't elaborate, and I'm hesitant to speak where Paul doesn't. There are, however, a few clues we can glean that might help us figure it out. First, let's think about the word itself. The word is *apostasia*. We get the word "apostasy" from it, which means falling away from the faith or abandoning one's allegiance to Christ. This is the same idea here.[20] The word also occurs in the book of Acts. Here Paul is told of a rumor going around about him, that some were saying that he taught Jews to abandon the Mosaic law: "you teach all the Jews who are among the Gentiles to forsake [*apostasian*] Moses" (Acts 21:21).[21]

Paul teaches that, sometime right before Christ returns, a significant falling away from the faith will occur.[22] In other words, people

---

20. It's also possible to understand the word to have *political*, and not just *religious*, connotations (Bruce, *1 & 2 Thessalonians*, 166). Indeed, in the ancient world, it would be inconceivable to separate the two. But this would not permit unrestrained speculation about the vocation of the future man of lawlessness. Moreover, the emphasis, given the context, seems to be on leading people away from the Christian faith, thus on the *religious* aspect. On this, see Malherbe, *Thessalonians*, 418; Green, *Letter to the Thessalonians*, 307.

21. See also the discussion in Heinrich Schlier, "Ἀφίστημι, Ἀποστασία, Διχοστασία," *TDNT* 1:512–14, esp. 513–14.

22. As Hoekema says, this refers to a "final, climactic apostasy just before the end-time." He adds, "It should be noted, however, that this apostasy will be an intensification and culmination

from within the church will abandon their devotion to Christ.[23] I don't think the apostasy is an event separated from the revealing of the man of lawlessness. This person is the one who leads people away from Christ. He destroys people's faith. He doesn't do this by wiping people's faith clean, leaving them with an atheistic or secularist mindset. He fights against the church by sitting in the temple, claiming to be God and thus replacing Christ with himself as the object of worship (2 Thess 2:4).

THE TEMPLE

What does Paul mean by "temple"? Some think this is a reference to a rebuilt Jewish temple.[24] Paul wrote this letter well before the destruction of the temple, and one might think that such a *physical* temple is what he has in mind here. I suspect, though, that Paul means something else. From his letters, we know Paul believes the church is the true temple of God (1 Cor 3:16–17; 6:19; 2 Cor 6:16; Eph 2:21–22). Most likely, this is what he means here. So when Paul says "he takes his seat in the temple of God, proclaiming himself to be God," he means the man of lawlessness works within the church (2 Thess 2:4). This is how he leads people away from the faith and into apostasy. It's an inside job. He "opposes" (*antikeimenos*) and "exalts himself against every so-called god or object of worship" by standing in the place of Christ (2:4).[25] In this sense, he is truly *anti*-christ. It would

---

of a rebellion which has already begun, since in verse 7 Paul says, 'For the mystery of lawlessness is already at work.' We may see a parallel, therefore, between this sign and the sign of tribulation: both are evident throughout the present age but come to a climactic and final form just before Christ returns" (*Bible and the Future*, 153).

23. See the discussion in Green, *Letters to the Thessalonians*, 307; see also Hoekema, *Bible and the Future*, 153.

24. See, e.g., Hagee, *Beginning of the End*, 128–29, 141–43.

25. Here Paul alludes to Dan 11:36, a text that originally spoke about Antiochus Epiphanes IV: "And the king shall do as he wills. He shall exalt himself and magnify himself above every god, and shall speak astonishing things against the God of gods. He shall prosper till the indignation is accomplished; for what is decreed shall be done." See also "the little horn" in Dan 7:8, as well as 7:20–25. On this, see the discussion in Bruce, *1 & 2 Thessalonians*, 168, 177; see also Green, *Letters to the Thessalonians*, 310.

not be unreasonable to interpret this as a replay of the abomination of desolation of the first-century temple. Perhaps Jesus's discussion in Matthew 24 does in fact contain another layer of meaning.

Paul is perplexed that he must remind the Thessalonians about the events surrounding the man of lawlessness. "Do you not remember that when I was still with you I told you these things?" (2 Thess 2:5). Paul must have spoken with them about these issues previously. This statement also suggests that his teaching on the man of lawlessness and events surrounding his appearance was in his mind so thorough that he expected them to remember it.[26] Perhaps we can conclude, then, that such teaching was common. From what we can tell, early Christian teaching about the rise of a sinister force, embodied in one individual at the end of the age, was well known and perhaps prolific (compare 1 John 2:18; 4:3).

MORE DETAILS

In the next passage (2 Thess 2:6–12), Paul provides a bit more detail about this sinister person and what empowers him. Paul says someone (or something) is restraining the man of lawlessness so that he doesn't show up before his time. He assumes the Thessalonians know the identity of this restrainer (2:6–7). Clearly, he and the Thessalonians have talked about this before (2:5). Perhaps he doesn't feel the need to get into the particulars again. Whoever, or whatever, the restrainer is, we can be sure that the restrainer is somehow connected to God's will and plan.[27] The point is that God is in control of the situation. This offers comfort and assurance to the Thessalonians.

---

26. Green says, "The question [of 2:5] implies that the church already had sufficient instruction to evaluate and reject the teaching that had so moved them and put them in turmoil. What they needed to do was simply to remember and apply the apostolic instruction, as is frequently the case in the battle against error (Jude 3)" (*Letters to the Thessalonians*, 313).

27. John Hagee thinks the restrainer is the Holy Spirit. When the rapture occurs, he says, every believer will be taken to heaven, thus leaving the earth without a restrainer—the Holy Spirit, who dwells within the very Christians who have been raptured. The rapture, therefore, allows for the man of lawlessness to be revealed (*Beginning of the End*, 106). There are numerous problems with views such as Hagee's. See, e.g., the discussion in Brown and Keener, *Not*

SATANIC EMPOWERMENT

The man of lawlessness is not autonomous. He doesn't act alone, nor does he act without influence. He is in fact empowered by Satan. "The coming [*parousia*] of the lawless one is by the activity of Satan with all power and false signs and wonders" (2 Thess 2:9). This could mean he will perform real signs and wonders, but they will be nonetheless false in the sense that they will be intended to lead people away from the truth. On the other hand, this could mean these signs and wonders will be fabricated—made to look as if they are real. Of course, Satan could empower him to do both.[28] Either way, his aim will be "wicked deception" (2:10). His "coming," which the word parousia suggests, is itself a knockoff of Jesus's own parousia.[29] The man of lawlessness is therefore a deceitful copycat.

God allows all of this to happen to "those who are perishing" because they have "refused to love the truth and so be saved" (2:10). In fact, the text says, "God sends them a strong delusion, so that they may believe what is false" (2:11). God does not do this because he doesn't want them saved, and God is neither in league with nor has the same plans as Satan (perish the thought!). To the contrary, it is because these people have chosen not to "believe the truth but had pleasure in unrighteousness" (2:12). Because they have opted for a life without the God of truth, God has confirmed their decision by giving them what they want.[30] He uses the man of lawlessness as an instrument of judgment.

Afraid, 139–41, 155–56. On various views regarding the identity of the restrainer, see Malherbe, *Thessalonians*, 432–33.

28. See also Malherbe (*Thessalonians*, 425), who offers three possibilities for how to understand "false" in 2:9. It could refer to the miracles' (1) "origin" ("they belong to the realm of him who is false") or (2) to their "quality" ("they are not truly miracles") or (3) to their "intention" ("to convince people of falsehood"). Malherbe dismisses (2), is open to the possibility of (1) being part of the equation, but in the end opts for (3). In my opinion, it's possible a little of everything is in view.

29. Bruce rightly says, "The false Christ has his solemn Parousia or, as we might call it (remembering the title of that proto-Antichrist, Antiochus Epiphanes), his 'epiphany.' (From the time of Gaius Caligula onward, ἐπιφάνεια [*epiphaneia*] is used of an emperor's parousia, with the implication that his visit is a 'manifestation' of divinity.) The use of παρουσία [*parousia*] here probably suggests a parody of Christ's Parousia (v 8)" (*1 & 2 Thessalonians*, 173).

30. "It is because of their refusal to love the truth that God acts in the way he does. God's action is thus in consequence of theirs" (Malherbe, *Thessalonians*, 426; see also 427).

But the man of lawlessness will come to an end. He will be destroyed, says Paul, at the coming of Jesus.[31] It will be an easy victory. The man of lawlessness, even with his satanic "power and false signs and wonders," is no match for the Lord of lords (2:9). Jesus will defeat him "with the breath of his mouth and bring [him] to nothing by the appearance of his coming" (2:8).[32] In other words, Jesus just shows up and starts talking. The end.

WHAT ABOUT THE BEAST?

I have already discussed the Beast's identity in chapter 3, where I argue that the Beast represents the first-century Roman Empire, particularly Nero as the archetypal symbol of its wickedness. I also mentioned there that the Beast could not be relegated to just Nero or the empire. As an apocalyptic symbol, the Beast is a fluid one. It can represent anything—and everything—that deliberately and overtly seeks to defy the kingdom of God. While I am convinced John had Rome in mind when he talked about the Beast, I am equally convinced his intent was to include in that symbol all of Satan's inspired antichrists. This would include *the* Antichrist and Paul's man of lawlessness.

It is interesting to compare the demise of the man of lawlessness with how John describes the overthrow of the Beast and false prophet.

Then I saw heaven opened, and behold, a white horse! The one sitting on it is called Faithful and True, and in righteousness he judges and makes war. His eyes are like a flame of fire, and on his head are many diadems, and he has a name written that no one knows but himself. He is clothed in a robe dipped in blood, and the name by which he is called is The Word of God. And the armies of heaven, arrayed in fine linen, white and pure, were following him on white horses. *From his mouth comes a sharp sword* with which to strike down the nations, and he will

---

31. His inevitable demise (2:8) is echoed in his name, "the son of destruction" (2:3; Malherbe, *Thessalonians*, 419); see also Green, *Letters to the Thessalonians*, 308–9.

32. This text recalls Isa 11:4 LXX (Bruce, *1 & 2 Thessalonians*, 172).

rule them with a rod of iron. He will tread the winepress of the
fury of the wrath of God the Almighty. ... And I saw the beast
and the kings of the earth with their armies gathered to make
war against him who was sitting on the horse and against his
army. *And the beast was captured, and with it the false prophet
who in its presence had done the signs by which he deceived those
who had received the mark of the beast and those who worshiped
its image. These two were thrown alive into the lake of fire
that burns with sulfur. And the rest were slain by the sword that
came from the mouth of him who was sitting on the horse,* and all
the birds were gorged with their flesh. (Rev 19:11–15, 19–21)

In this passage, the person on the white horse is named "The Word
of God," which is a clear reference to Jesus (compare John 1:1). He is
depicted with a sword protruding from his mouth, a symbolic way
of describing the power of his word. In fact, as God's word in flesh,
Jesus's mere presence is sufficient to overcome any enemies he has.
The text above does not say explicitly that Jesus uses his words to
defeat the Beast and the false prophet. Though the text says he defeats
the nations with his word, it states the Beast and false prophet were
"captured," leaving no indication how (19:20). That said, we are safe
to read between the lines. The only weapon mentioned is the "sword"
of his mouth, and it is safe to assume that this is the manner in which
the archetypal foes are defeated as well.

If that is correct, it's very similar to how Paul describes the defeat
of the man of lawlessness. "And then the lawless one will be revealed,
whom the Lord Jesus will kill with the breath of his mouth and bring
to nothing by the appearance of his coming" (2 Thess 2:8).[33] Both John
and Paul describe a final nemesis being destroyed at the return of Christ.
Both depict the victory as a result of Jesus simply speaking. Moreover,
just as the man of lawlessness arrives with "power" as the result of "the

---

33. Note that "breath" is a translation of *pneumati*, from *pneuma*, which can be translated
"spirit" or "Spirit." Compare "the sword of the Spirit [*pneumatos*], which is the word of God,"
in Eph 6:17.

activity of Satan" (2 Thess 2:9), so also the Beast is granted "power" by the dragon (Rev 13:3), who is described as "Satan" (Rev 12:9).[34]

There are no direct similarities between the Beast and the Antichrist. The reason is that so little is said about the Antichrist in 1 and 2 John. But there are similarities between the way John describes the Antichrist and the way Paul describes the man of lawlessness. The man of lawlessness is clearly an individual person who is coming in the future (2 Thess 2:3). But Paul says that, even in his own time, there is a "mystery of lawlessness" that is "already at work" (2:7). This is very similar to John's Antichrist: he is an individual person who is coming in the future, and yet the "spirit of the antichrist" is alive and well in the first century (1 John 2:18; 4:3). Moreover, Paul associates "deception" and false teaching ("the rebellion," *apostasia*) with the man of lawlessness (2 Thess 2:3, 10–11). John also connects the Antichrist (and antichrists) with false teaching, lies, and deception (1 John 2:18–27; 4:1–6; 2 John 4–11).

Another interesting similarity is how both John and Paul reveal that their readers had already received teaching about the Antichrist and man of lawlessness, respectively. John states his readers "have heard" that Antichrist was coming (1 John 2:18).[35] Likewise, Paul says he taught the Thessalonians about the man of lawlessness previous to his writing 2 Thessalonians. He is even surprised they so easily forgot about it. Or perhaps he is amazed they failed to process it with respect to their fears about having missed the coming of Jesus (see 2 Thess 2:1, 5). Either way, Paul's shock likewise suggests that teaching on the subject was part of the church's primary instruction. This similarity with John's discussion about the Antichrist/antichrists is possible evidence they are speaking about the same final nemesis. At the very least, it's not unreasonable to think they are.

---

34. This insight comes from Bruce, who says, "The energizing of the man of lawlessness by Satan has its analogue in Rev 13:2, where the beast from the abyss (the persecuting empire) receives 'his power and his throne and great authority' from the great red dragon" (*1 & 2 Thessalonians*, 173).

35. John says the same regarding "the spirit of the antichrist" (1 John 4:3).

HOW ARE THE ANTICHRIST, MAN OF LAWLESSNESS, AND BEAST RELATED?

There is ample evidence to suggest Paul's man of lawlessness and John's Antichrist are the same person. According to Anthony Hoekema, most commentators equate the two.[36] Even though John gives very little detail, Paul's version fills in some of the gaps. Hoekema says,

> What is ... not wholly clear in John's teaching about the antichrist becomes clear here [in 2 Thess 2]: there will be a final, personal antichrist before the day of the Lord comes. Though some have suggested that we should read Paul in the light of John, and others have implied that we should read John in the light of Paul, I believe that we should take both approaches into account. There is no basic conflict between these two approaches since, as we have seen, John leaves room for the coming of a future personal antichrist, and Paul recognizes that antichristian forces are already at work in the world (v. 7).[37]

I agree with this approach. Each passage helps interpret the other. And while it is true Paul provides more information than John does about the Antichrist, we must admit that Paul isn't exactly forthcoming on every detail either. Nowhere does he tell us how long the man of lawlessness will be on the scene. We get no indication about his ethnicity, citizenship, or age.

Paul does seem to suggest the man of lawlessness works within the church, which might suggest he poses as a Christian. He does his dastardly deeds in the temple, which again may be a reference to believers. He deceives and leads an apostasy—a rebellion from the true faith of Jesus Christ. He may initially be a confessing Christian, that is, as an *anti*-christian (taking "anti" to mean "in the place of"). This is why I mentioned at the end of the last chapter that those evangelicals who look outside the church for the Antichrist have perhaps

---

36. Hoekema, *Bible and the Future*, 154, 159.
37. Hoekema, *Bible and the Future*, 159.

been looking in the wrong place. The final nemesis may be especially appealing to some Christians.

What about the Beast? Is he the final Antichrist, the man of lawlessness? As we saw above, Revelation 19 says there is a Beast (and false prophet) present when Jesus returns.[38] This is similar to how the man of lawlessness is described (2 Thess 2:8). Like the man of lawlessness, the Beast is also said to be empowered by Satan (see 2 Thess 2:9; Rev 12:9, 17; 13:1–18). Paul describes the man of lawlessness as the center of worship, which is again similar to the first Beast, who receives worship from people at the instigation of the second Beast (false prophet; see 2 Thess 2:4; Rev 13:4, 12; 19:20, respectively).

In Revelation, the Beast is a symbol of Satan's nefarious work on earth, and for John this was manifested in the first-century Roman imperial system. So we can't divorce the Beast from its first-century context. Yet, John says the Beast is alive when Christ returns, which is far removed from the first century. Is John saying that first-century Rome—or one of her first-century emperors—will be around when Jesus returns? Obviously, no. We need a deeper understanding of the picture Revelation is painting of the Beast.

Most likely, John is telescoping a far distant event (the return of Christ) into his first-century discussion so that he can describe the demise of the Roman imperial system. This has the effect of reassuring his first-century readers that God will judge beastly Rome, giving confidence to their belief that the empire's reign is only temporary. John himself may very well have thought Jesus would return in the first century and literally bring about the end of Rome. Every Christian of every era rightly anticipates the Lord's return. But, with the benefit of hindsight, we know Jesus did not return in John's time. Indeed, *we* are still waiting. But when Jesus does return, he will put an end to every Satan-inspired work, including that of the final Antichrist.

By describing it the way he does, John allows some flexibility in how we interpret the identity of the Beast. It gives us space for

---

38. The false prophet is the second Beast of Rev 13:11–18 (see Rev 19:20).

understanding how Revelation's Beast is *both* a reference to first-century Rome *and* a symbol for Satan's ongoing nefarious work throughout church history. The sinister activity of Satan has continued beyond the first century and into the second, third, and fourth centuries—all the way up until the present era. Satan's Beast, as well as his mark, continues to be manifested in various ways today. This will be true up until Christ returns and destroys all of Satan's work. The meaning, therefore, is not so much that Jesus will come back to destroy first-century Rome, but that Jesus will come back to destroy the Beast, which in the first century was Rome but in later centuries represents whatever sinister person or institution is alive when Jesus returns.

In light of this, it's probably not helpful to say the Beast is the Antichrist. It's better to say the Antichrist is the Beast. The Beast is only paradigmatic of the final Antichrist. We probably should not see any one-to-one correspondence between the two, either. In other words, we shouldn't necessarily expect the Antichrist to mimic every little thing John describes about Revelation's Beast. Just because, for example, John's beastly emperor was located on the literal seven-hilled city of Rome does not mean we should be looking for the Antichrist to have political offices in Rome. I'm not saying this won't happen. I'm just saying it's not necessary that it does. When it comes to the end times, especially in regard to the final nemesis, we should always be hesitant to speculate about the details where the Scripture is silent. Again, there's a lot we can't know.

Generally speaking, however, what we can know is this. The final nemesis will lead people into rebellion against God and his laws, thus earning the name "man of law*lessness*." By doing so, he will persecute and tempt the church, mirroring the same beastly qualities as imperial Rome of the first century. Like the prostitute in Revelation 17–18, the Antichrist will tempt people to fall into spiritual drunkenness and lawless immorality (see Rev 17:1–2; 18:1–3). But again, every antichrist of every era exhibits many of the same qualities of Revelation's Beast. They often mimic Rome's insatiable decadence, lust for conquest, and gross immorality. In the texts examined above, we can say the same will be true for the anti-Christian man of lawlessness. But his work (however long it lasts) will come to an abrupt end when Jesus returns (2 Thess 2:8). It is in this sense that Jesus will defeat every Satan-inspired beastly apparition—including the final Beast—when he returns (Rev 19:11–21).

WE DON'T KNOW THE TIMING

We can't know when any of this is going to happen. There have been, currently are, and will be many antichrists (see again 1 John 2:18, 22; 2 John 7). The "spirit of the antichrist" and the "mystery of lawlessness" are already here and have been for a long time (1 John 4:3; 2 Thess 2:7, respectively). We should not be surprised when these sinister forces show up, persecuting and tempting the church to unfaithfulness. It happens all the time—in every era throughout history.[39]

But it will not go on forever. There will be a *final* nemesis. But even if we were to see a person rise and lead many people astray in our lifetime, we could not be certain this person is the final Antichrist. The only way we can know with certainty is after the fact. Only when Jesus suddenly appears and destroys this antichrist will we know that he was the final Antichrist. As Craig Keener says, "What will finally indicate that we have witnessed the final Antichrist will be Jesus' return to wipe him out."[40] In the meantime, we should not be surprised when we see antichrists routinely come on the scene. Because Satan himself does not know when Christ will return (Matt 24:36), he can't know who the final Antichrist will be, either. That's why he always has one lined up.[41] Through every tribulation, through every antichrist (including the final Antichrist), Christians have a duty to be faithful to the true Christ.

---

39. "Since John sees these 'many antichrists' in the world already, he concludes that we are now, in this present era, in 'the last hour.' We can thus expect to continue to find antichristian powers and persons in every era of the church of Jesus Christ until his Second Coming" (Hoekema, *Bible and the Future*, 158).

40. Keener, *Revelation*, 360; see also Brown and Keener, *Not Afraid*, 177.

41. Brown and Keener, *Not Afraid*, 176 (see also 130).

As I mentioned previously, the ongoing tribulation might develop into something worse in the future than what the worldwide church is *currently* experiencing. But if, or when, this happens, we can't speak definitively that *this* is the final trial. It could be yet another trial like what the world has experienced in the past. In the moment of that trial, we can't know there won't be something *worse* in the future. Again, the only way to know whether it is the final trial is when Jesus shows up to put an end to it. After Jesus appears, then—and only then—will we be able to properly interpret the events leading up to his return. In the meantime, we Christians are called to be faithful through every period of tribulation, maintain our witness, and refuse to compromise our love for Jesus.

CONCLUSION: WHAT NOW?

In this book, you've traveled back in time. You sat on the Mount of Olives, listening closely to Jesus as he predicted the temple's destruction. You followed him into Caiaphas's chambers and watched as he left, riding victoriously on the clouds. You saw the temple's destruction and the focusing of God's presence in a new temple—the church. This temple will never be destroyed, no matter how bad the tribulation. You saw this firsthand when you gazed into the faces of faithful Christians who refused to worship Caesar's image. In a world of imperial propaganda, they bore witness to the gospel boldly, confidently, and unwaveringly. Despite constant threats and continual dangers, these early Christians were full of kingdom hope. They knew the Beast was real, but he was no match for the Lamb who was slain. They were a church that endured joyfully because they knew their future was secure. They might not have known all the details about that future, but that didn't matter. It was enough to know that God's story—and their story—would end in glory.

I hope you've seen that a biblical perspective of the end times will lead us to peace, not panic—to hope, not horror. Even when we find ourselves face to face with the Beast, we are unafraid. An eschatology that is founded on Scripture will never create alarm or fear—even when the world turns upside down.

Because we know the end is secure, the need to anticipate every detail about the future can fall to the wayside. A Christ-centered perspective on the end times will not drive us to speculate about the final events—especially where the Bible is silent or vague. Instead, it will lead us to faithfulness and peace *despite not knowing the details.*

It will give us peace in the things we can know and contentment for the things we can't.

As we close this book, I want to leave you with a few thoughts that summarize all that we have learned.

FOCUS ON THE LAMB, NOT THE BEAST

Biblical eschatology is about the Lamb, not the Beast. That means the Lamb should be our focus. The Lamb is the object of our worship, so his work ought to take center stage. When we spend so much time speculating about what the Antichrist will be like, what he will do, and when he will show up, we communicate to others that he, not Jesus, is the main topic. But as Christians we are to fear only God, not anyone else.

When we focus on evil things, our minds grow paranoid about the future. This isn't what biblical eschatology intends for us to do. It isn't healthy. Paul tells us to dwell on things that are good: "Whatever is true, whatever is honorable, whatever is just, whatever is pure, whatever is lovely, whatever is commendable, if there is any excellence, if there is anything worthy of praise, think about these things" (Phil 4:8).

This doesn't mean we can't study the negative side of eschatology—for example, the mark of the Beast, tribulation, Antichrist. I'm not against this (I've written a book about these things, after all!). But we only study these things in light of the good promises of Jesus. The mark of the Beast should remind us that we have been marked with the seal of the Lamb. The tribulation should remind us that God will preserve us through tribulation. And our study of the Antichrist should always focus on his defeat. He's not that spectacular, to be honest. He's a pitiful parody of Christ—a laughingstock and cheap imitator. Our focus should be on Jesus, the one who loves us and protects us. He's the star of the show, not the Antichrist.

YOU DON'T HAVE TO KNOW EVERY
DETAIL ABOUT THE FUTURE

I wish I knew more about how the end times will unfold. But the fact is, there's a lot we can't know. We need to be content with this. When the Bible is vague or ambiguous about the future, we shouldn't rush to fill in the gaps or speak where the Bible doesn't.

The desire to know details about the future is common to us all. Even the disciples struggled with this. In the last chapter of John's Gospel, Jesus engages Peter in a soul-searching conversation. Peter had recently denied his Lord three times, and here Jesus seeks to restore their relationship. At the end of their discussion, Jesus prophesies over Peter, saying,

> "Truly, truly, I say to you, when you were young, you used to dress yourself and walk wherever you wanted, but when you are old, you will stretch out your hands, and another will dress you and carry you where you do not want to go." (This he said to show by what kind of death he was to glorify God.) And after saying this he said to him, "Follow me." (John 21:18–19)

According to church tradition, Peter died by crucifixion. Jesus seems to refer to something like that here—albeit cryptically. In a very real sense, Peter is offered a glimpse into the future. Jesus didn't have to share any of this, but for whatever reason, it's something he thought Peter ought to know.

This makes Peter curious, though. He wants to know *more* details about the future. Seeing his fellow disciple John, Peter asks Jesus about his fate: "Lord, what about this man?" (21:21). Jesus responds, "If it is my will that he remain until I come, what is that to you? You follow me!" (21:22). Jesus's answer suggests Peter was wondering whether John would live to see the final events—the return of Jesus. Would John be part of the final generation? Jesus refuses to give an answer. It's none of Peter's business. What matters is that Peter focuses on his own calling.

Interestingly, a rumor began to spread among the early Christians that John would be alive when Jesus returned (21:23). This is humorous. Perhaps the earliest Christians were just like many of us today, quick to shout where Jesus has not spoken. In response to this rumor, John adds an insightful comment: "So the saying spread abroad among the brothers that this disciple was not to die; *yet Jesus did not say to him that he was not to die*, but, 'If it is my will that he remain until I come, what is that to you?'" (John 21:23).

John is a careful listener. Jesus never said he wouldn't die, but only that such a topic is none of Peter's business. In doing so, Jesus left open the possibility that John would be part of the final generation that would see Jesus's return. But he never said one way or the other. John recognized this. Such speculation was none of *his* business, either. So, even he refuses to think any further on the matter. In the next verse, in fact, John moves on to more important matters, saying, "This is the disciple who is bearing witness about these things, and who has written these things, and we know that his testimony is true" (John 21:24). Because John didn't preoccupy himself with *future* things that were above his pay grade, he was freed up to focus on the *present* task at hand, namely, to be a faithful witness to Jesus.

Perhaps there's something here for us to learn. Like John, it's possible you and I will be alive to witness the second coming. But it's also possible we won't. Jesus doesn't say. Contrary to some prophecy teachers, we *cannot* know that we are part of the final generation. What Jesus calls us to do is to follow him—to be faithful witnesses in the present.

Let's be content not knowing the details.

DON'T BE AFRAID TO ASK QUESTIONS

When I was a young Christian, I was fascinated with the theology of the Left Behind series. I also listened attentively to famous megachurch pastors and prophecy teachers talk about the end times. They were so certain about everything. They had all the events lined out—detail upon detail. Everything happening in the Middle East was a fulfillment of prophecy, they said, just like God's word predicted. The United Nations was a precursor to the Antichrist's worldwide government. Microchip technology was the mechanism through which everyone would be branded, marked with the name of the Antichrist. All the natural disasters, all the wars and rumors of wars, were signs that we were the final generation. No question about it. The rapture was imminent, the Antichrist was alive, his government was in place—and we were constantly on the lookout.

But then I started to ask questions.

Where did the Bible talk about the rapture? Where did it say the Antichrist would show up after the church left the earth? What verse said the mark of the Beast was a computer chip or a barcode? Where in the Bible did it teach that the great tribulation would take place in the future? What passage in Revelation said 666 was part of a prophecy about a one-world currency?

As I began to ask these questions to myself, as well as pose them to fellow Christians who subscribed to this sort of eschatology, I discovered something significant: *none of us knew where the Bible spoke about these topics.* As it turned out, we were all reliant on modern prophecy teachers to tell us what to believe. It never occurred to us to ask questions, to raise doubts, to notice problems with these views. Sadly, we were never trained to ask questions, but only to listen.

That's a problem.

The truth is, we need to ask more questions. We should not just listen. When we read books written by popular prophecy teachers or listen to their sermons, we need to ask where they got their information. Do their beliefs come from Scripture, or are they simply making assumptions? When they present their views, are they making arguments from Scripture, or are they simply stating what they believe? Christians should learn to observe the difference between a *statement of a belief* and an *argument for a belief.* We need to think critically and carefully about such things. We can start by asking questions.

In fact, start with this book. Do I make arguments *from* Scripture, or do I merely make statements? Do I base my views *on* the Bible's teachings, or do I simply present my own assumptions? Do I provide *context* for the verses I quote, or do I flippantly toss out random prooftexts? Asking questions and seeking answers is the route to truth.

FIND THE STORY BEHIND
THE BIBLICAL TEXT

When you study end-times passages in Scripture, don't settle for reading a verse or two. Read the entire chapter of the passage you are studying. In fact, you may even need to read the entire book. This will give the text some context, and it will help you understand what the passage is talking about.

But there's more to context than just reading the verses before and after the passage you are studying. You must do more than simply look *around* the text. You have to get *behind* the text, too. You must realize that the passage itself was written within a historical setting—a different time and place from what you are familiar with. For example, to understand how 1 Thessalonians 4:13–18 did not teach the rapture, we had to enter the world of the first century. By investigating the historical background of certain words in that text, we learned that Paul could not have been teaching that Christians would be secretly caught up into heaven. Instead, he taught that at the "coming" of Christ, Christians would go out "to meet the Lord in the air" and then escort him back to earth—as was customary to do with the arrival of royal dignitaries in Paul's day (4:15, 17). The fact is, the New Testament is an ancient text written by ancient authors to ancient people. As such, it is embedded within an ancient culture, full of ancient customs, assumptions, and traditions. Learning about these things is what it means to get *behind* the text.

Sometimes we neglect to do this. We are so preoccupied with reading *in front of the text* (that is, with only our own assumptions in mind) that we effectively mute the text. We rob it of its voice. This happens a lot when people study eschatology. They tend to read the Bible from the standpoint of current events, interpreting end-times passages through the lens of the latest geopolitical controversy. Our readings often impose our own modern, Western (and sometimes American) political assumptions onto the text. This isn't helpful.

I'm not suggesting there isn't a place for reading the Bible in light of *our* situation and assumptions. In fact, we can't help but do this. We always read texts from the standpoint of our assumptions. None of us are truly objective. But we cannot do this without considering the text's own assumptions. In other words, if we want to get in *front* of the text, we need to get *behind* it, too. The only way the Bible can speak to our own times is when we let the Bible speak from *its* own time. If Scripture is to have a voice in the twenty-first century, *its* voice must be spoken in the tongue of its original writer.

REMEMBER TO KEEP WAITING

Eschatology is the study of the end times. As we've seen, the end times is the current era in which we find ourselves. It's been around for two thousand years, ever since Jesus ascended to the Father. One day, he will return. That's one prophecy that has yet to be fulfilled. But what are we supposed to do in the meantime? The answer is simple: *we wait.*

But what does it mean to wait? Does it mean to sit around and speculate about the future? Does it mean we become so infatuated with tomorrow that we become no use for today? I think we all know that such attitudes are not pleasing to the Lord.

We see this best in a parable Jesus gives in Matthew 25, the parable of the talents (25:14–30). In this story, Jesus describes what the Christian life should be like between his first and second comings. He speaks of a certain property owner who, before going on a long trip, hands over some of his money to three of his servants. To one servant, he gives five talents; to a second servant, he gives two talents; and to his third servant, he gives one talent. He entrusts his money to them so they can invest it while he is gone. After the owner returns, he discovers the first servant worked hard, earning five more talents. The second servant did quite well, too. He labored faithfully to produce two more talents. The owner is quite pleased with both workers.

But when he comes to his third servant (to whom he gave one talent), he discovers something disheartening. That servant has proven lazy, never putting the owner's money to use. Instead, this servant chose to play it safe. So, he buried the talent in the ground and gave it back to the owner when he returned. The owner isn't amused, rebuking the servant for his laziness and for his utter disregard for the job. The servant was entrusted to do something profitable with the time his master gave him. Yet, he sat around and did nothing. He just passed the time, waiting on his master to return.

Sadly, this describes the attitude of many Christians today. We know our Lord has entrusted us with spiritual gifts, and yet we do nothing—or very little—with them. We play it safe by passively *waiting* until the second coming. Thankfully, there is another way to wait for the Lord's return. Instead of waiting *passively*, we can wait *actively*. We can choose to spend our days waiting for the Lord's return by mimicking the hard work of the first two servants. Instead of burying our talents, we can serve the kingdom by putting them to use.

In this parable, Jesus teaches us something important about what biblical eschatology ought to look like. It's not about a church wanting to *escape earth*, but about being faithful *on the earth*. It's not about being preoccupied with details of the *future*, but about being fixated on the *present* task at hand. In other words, eschatology cannot be about entering into speculations about what might happen at the end of time. It's about faithfully carrying out God's will on earth as it is in heaven in the present time.

What made the first two servants so successful in their work was that they didn't sit around musing about the fine details of their lord's return. They didn't build towers from which they could peer into the distance for signs of when their master would return. They didn't draw up timelines or charts or calendars so they could map out all the details of their master's return. Such speculation would have distracted them from what they already knew. It was sufficient for them to know simply that he would return. They had a job to do until he came again.

In the same vein, I wonder whether some Christians have missed the entire point of eschatology. Spilling so much ink pontificating about what might happen in the future distracts us from today's task. Suppose one morning I told my children that, after I come home from work, I would take them to Disney World—the happiest place on earth, they say. In the meantime, I leave them a list of things to do so they're ready to go as soon as I get home: clean the house, finish the dishes, wash their clothes, pack their bags. All day long, they would work with excitement—anticipating my return home. In the same way, we should actively wait for Jesus's return.

It's okay to delve into what the Bible says about eschatology. We can even explore the fine details, as the Bible permits. But this doesn't give us permission to engage in speculations beyond what the Bible clearly tells us. We aren't permitted to speak with certainty about things we can't possibly know. Some of us can get so fixated on mapping out an eschatological timetable that incorporates *those* events in the Middle East or *this* natural disaster in the southern hemisphere or *that* political development in the United States that we stray far from the Bible's message and become distracted (not to mention anxious!). As a result, the world looks at us with smirks and eye rolls. Instead, the church ought to tread carefully in these matters. Our witness is at stake. Let's be energized by what we know: that Christ will return and make all things new. Though it means hard work in the meantime—through toil, trial, and tribulation—we can be energized by the peace and joy that comes with knowing Christ will return.

When that day comes, our Lord will return not to take us to another place but to bring to us a gift that will satisfy our deepest longings and fulfill our innermost dreams. He will bring to earth the new Jerusalem, a place where tears cannot be found, where all sickness is healed, where strife has ceased, where hate has been expunged, where relationships are healed, and where death is no more. In the end, heaven will be the happiest place on earth. And actually, it's not the end at all.

In fact, it's just the beginning.

ACKNOWLEDGMENTS

I could not have written this book without the support and encouragement of my friends and family. I would like to thank Joe McGee, Jonathan and Kelly Hellmuth, Dena Herring, and my mother, Jeanette Deese, for reading portions of this book and offering invaluable thoughts along the way. Many thanks are likewise due to New Life Bible Church, a church family that is an unceasing source of joy to me and my family.

I am indebted to Dr. Tavis Bohlinger for the kind invitation to write a series of articles on the end times for the Logos blog. In fact, if it weren't for him, this project would never have gotten off the ground, as he was the first to pitch the idea of writing a book after those articles were published.

Words cannot express my gratitude to my editor, Elliot Ritzema, for his hard work on the manuscript that eventually became this book. His sharp eye and perceptiveness have been integral in molding the initial draft into something readable. I'm incredibly grateful for his many hours of investment in this book.

It goes without saying, but this book would not have been possible without the support of my wife, Tosha. She's constantly supporting me in my writing, offering encouragement and loving inspiration without fail. She's a treasure—the jewel of my heart and my lifelong friend. My kids, too, have always been my biggest fans, cheering me on as I worked on this book. Their laughs, their smiles, and their joy are contagious and inspiring. They are true gifts from God.

I've dedicated this book to each of my children (Isaac, Gracie, Hannah, and Simon) because I want them to see the hope we have in Jesus. No matter what they may encounter in this strange world, I want them to know that all things will be made right in the end—when the King returns. Indeed, come quickly, Lord Jesus!

BIBLIOGRAPHY

Aland, Barbara, et al., eds. *Novum Testamentum Graece*. 28th ed. Stuttgart: Deutsche Bibelgesellschaft, 2012.

Alter, Robert. *The Hebrew Bible: The Writings: A Translation with Commentary*. Vol. 3. New York: Norton, 2019.

Aune, David E. *Revelation 1–5*. WBC. Dallas: Word, 1997.

———. *Revelation 6–16*. WBC. Dallas: Thomas Nelson, 1998.

———. *Revelation 17–22*. WBC. Dallas: Thomas Nelson, 1998.

Bandy, Alan S. "Persecution and the Purpose of Revelation with Reference to Roman Jurisprudence." *BBR* 23 (2013): 377–98.

———. *The Prophetic Lawsuit in the Book of Revelation*. NTM. Sheffield: Sheffield Phoenix, 2010.

Bauckham, Richard. *The Theology of the Book of Revelation*. NTT. Cambridge: Cambridge University Press, 1993.

Beal, Timothy. *Revelation: A Biography*. Lives of Great Religious Books. Princeton: Princeton University Press, 2018.

Beale, G. K. *The Book of Revelation: A Commentary on the Greek Text*. NIGTC. Grand Rapids: Eerdmans, 1999.

Blumhofer, C. M. "Luke's Alteration of Joel 3.1–5 in Acts 2.17–21." *NTS* 62 (October 2016): 499–516.

Bock, Darrell L. *Acts*. BECNT. Grand Rapids: Baker Academic, 2007.

Brown, Michael L., and Craig S. Keener. *Not Afraid of the Antichrist: Why We Don't Believe in a Pre-tribulational Rapture*. Bloomington, MN: Chosen, 2019.

Bruce, F. F. *1 & 2 Thessalonians*. WBC. Waco, TX: Word, 1982.

Burke, Daniel. "How the 'Islamic Antichrist' Reflects Our Era's Anxieties." Religion News Service, February 6, 2013. https://religionnews. com/2013/02/06/how-the-antichrist-reflects-an-eras-anxities/.

Caird, G. B. *The Revelation of St. John the Divine.* New York: Harper & Row, 1966.

CBN News. "Pat Robertson Prophecy: Here's Who Will Win Election, Then End Times Prophecies Will Unfold." YouTube, 12:26, October 20, 2020. https://youtu.be/LAUbsx5iUFk.

Chisholm, Robert B. *Interpreting the Minor Prophets.* Grand Rapids: Zondervan, 1990.

Collins, John J. *Daniel: A Commentary on the Book of Daniel.* Minneapolis: Augsburg Fortress, 1993.

——. "Introduction: Towards the Morphology of a Genre." *Semeia* 14 (1979): 1–20.

——. "Sibylline Oracles." *OTP* 1:317–472.

deSilva, David A. *Discovering Revelation: Content, Interpretation, Reception.* DBT. Grand Rapids: Eerdmans, 2021.

——. *Introducing the Apocrypha: Message, Context, and Significance.* 2nd ed. Grand Rapids: Baker Academic, 2018.

——. *Unholy Allegiances: Heeding Revelation's Warning.* Peabody, MA: Hendrickson, 2013.

Dillard, Raymond. "Joel." Pages 239–313 in *The Minor Prophets: An Exegetical and Expository Commentary.* Edited by Thomas Edward McComiskey. Grand Rapids: Baker, 1992.

Elliger, K., and W. Rudolph, eds. *Biblia Hebraica Stuttgartensia.* 5th ed. Stuttgart: Deutsche Bibelgesellschaft, 1997.

Ferguson, Everett. *Church History, Volume 1: From Christ to Pre-Reformation: The Rise and Growth of the Church in Its Cultural, Intellectual, and Political Context.* Grand Rapids: Zondervan, 2005.

Foerster, Werner. "Ἀστήρ, Ἄστρον." *TDNT* 1:503–5.

France, R. T. *The Gospel of Matthew.* NICNT. Grand Rapids: Eerdmans, 2007.

Friesen, Steven J. *Imperial Cults and the Apocalypse of John: Reading Revelation in the Ruins.* New York: Oxford University Press, 2001.

Gaertringen, F. Frhr. Hiller von, ed. *Inschriften von Priene.* Berlin: Reimer, 1906.

Gleeson, Scott, and Asha C. Gilbert. "Some Say Covid-19 Vaccine Is the 'Mark of the Beast.' Is There a Connection to the Bible?" *USA Today*, September 27, 2021. https://www.usatoday.com/story/news/nation/2021/09/26/covid-vaccine-mark-beast-what-book-revelation-says/8255268002/.

Goldingay, John. *Daniel*. WBC. Rev. ed. Grand Rapids: Zondervan, 2019.

———. *Isaiah*. NIBC. Peabody, MA: Hendrickson, 2001.

Gorman, Michael J. *Reading Revelation Responsibly: Uncivil Worship and Witness: Following the Lamb into the New Creation*. Eugene, OR: Cascade, 2011.

Green, Gene L. *The Letters to the Thessalonians*. PNTC. Grand Rapids: Eerdmans, 2002.

Hagee, John. *Beginning of the End: The Assassination of Yitzhak Rabin and the Coming Antichrist*. Nashville: Thomas Nelson, 1996.

Hagee, Matt. *Your Guide to the Apocalypse: What You Should Know before the World Comes to an End*. Colorado Springs: WaterBrook, 2017.

Hagner, Donald A. *Matthew 14–28*. WBC. Dallas: Word, 1995.

Halsted, Matthew L. "The Covid Vaccine Has 666 Written All over It … and Why That Doesn't Matter According to Revelation." *The Logos Academic Blog*, May 18, 2020. https://www.logos.com/grow/the-covid-vaccine-has-666-written-all-over-it-and-why-that-doesnt-matter-according-to-revelation/.

———. "Monkeypox and the Plagues of Revelation: Is There a Connection?" *Word by Word*, October 7, 2022. https://www.logos.com/grow/hall-monkeypox-revelation/.

———. *Paul and the Meaning of Scripture: A Philosophical-Hermeneutic Approach to Paul's Use of the Old Testament in Romans*. Eugene, OR: Pickwick, 2022.

Heiser, Michael S. *The Unseen Realm: Recovering the Supernatural Worldview of the Bible*. Bellingham, WA: Lexham Press, 2015.

Hemer, Colin J. *The Letters to the Seven Churches of Asia in Their Local Setting*. Grand Rapids: Eerdmans, 1989.

Hitchcock, Mark. *101 Answers to the Most Asked Questions about the End Times*. Sisters, OR: Multnomah, 2001.

———. *The End: A Complete Overview of Bible Prophecy and the End of Days.* Carol Stream, IL: Tyndale House, 2012.

Hoekema, Anthony A. *The Bible and the Future.* Grand Rapids: Eerdmans, 1994.

Hollyfield, Amy. "According to The Book of Revelations the Anti-Christ ... Will Be a Man, in His 40s, of MUSLIM Descent ... Is It OBAMA??" PolitiFact, April 2, 2008. https://www.politifact.com/factchecks/2008/apr/02/chain-email/complete-distortion-of-the-bible/.

Jefferson, Thomas. "From Thomas Jefferson to Alexander Smyth, 17 January 1825." Founders Online, National Archives. https://founders.archives.gov/documents/Jefferson/98-01-02-4882.

Keener, Craig S. *Revelation.* NIVAC. Grand Rapids: Zondervan, 2000.

———. "Understanding Revelation." YouTube, June 5, 2017. https://www.youtube.com/watch?v=BIJRlQhWi5w&list=PLcuztqVj7ClA4PF1Z faylJTOT01sqpNpw&index=2.

———. "What Is the Mark of the Beast? Craig S. Keener Explains." YouTube, January 10, 2018. https://www.youtube.com/watch?v=r3eIWA9XS04.

Kim, Tae Hun. "The Anarthrous υἱὸς θεοῦ in Mark 15,39 and the Roman Imperial Cult." *Biblica* 79 (1998): 221–41.

Klauck, Hans-Josef. "Do They Never Come Back? *Nero Redivivus* and the Apocalypse of John." *CBQ* 63 (October 2001): 683–98.

Kraybill, J. Nelson. *Apocalypse and Allegiance: Worship, Politics, and Devotion in the Book of Revelation.* Grand Rapids: Brazos, 2010.

Lacocque, André. *The Book of Daniel.* Translated by David Pellauer. Atlanta: John Knox, 1979.

LaHaye, Tim. *Revelation Unveiled.* Rev. ed. Grand Rapids: Zondervan, 1999.

LaHaye, Tim, and Jerry B. Jenkins, *Are We Living in the End Times? Current Events Foretold in Scripture ... and What They Mean.* Updated and expanded ed. Carol Stream, IL: Tyndale House, 2011.

Lindsey, Hal. *Planet Earth—2000 A.D. Will Mankind Survive?* Palos Verdes, CA: Western Front, 1994.

Luther, Martin. *Word and Sacrament 1*. Edited by E. Theodore Bachman. Luther's Works 35. Philadelphia: Muhlenberg, 1960.

MacArthur, John. *Because the Time Is Near*. Chicago: Moody, 2007.

———. *John 12–21*. Chicago: Moody, 2008.

Malherbe, Abraham J. *The Letters to the Thessalonians*. AB. New York: Doubleday, 2000.

Newport, Kenneth G. C. *Apocalypse and Millennium: Studies in Biblical Eisegesis*. Cambridge: Cambridge University Press, 2000.

Nolland, John. *The Gospel of Matthew*. NIGTC. Grand Rapids: Eerdmans, 2005.

Oepke, Albrecht. "Παρουσία, Πάρειμι." *TDNT* 5:858–71.

Osborne, Grant R. *Revelation*. BECNT. Grand Rapids: Baker, 2002.

———. *Revelation: Verse by Verse*. ONTC. Bellingham, WA: Lexham Press, 2016.

Parker, Floyd O. "'Our Lord and God' in Rev 4,11: Evidence for the Late Date of Revelation." *Biblica* 82 (2001): 207–31.

Peterson, Erik. "Ἀπάντησις." *TDNT* 1:380–81.

Pliny. *Letters and Panegyiricus*. Translated by Betty Radice. Edited by G. P. Goold. 2 vols. LCL. Cambridge: Harvard University Press, 1975.

Rahlfs, Alfred, and Robert Hanhart. *Septuaginta: Id est Vetus Testamentum graece iuxta LXX interpretes*. Editio altera. Stuttgart: Deutsche Bibelgesellschaft, 2006.

Schlier, Heinrich. "Ἀφίστημι, Ἀποστασία, Διχοστασία." *TDNT* 1:512–14.

Smith, Ralph L. *Micah–Malachi*. WBC. Waco, TX: Word, 1984.

Smith-Christopher, Daniel L. *Daniel*. NIB. Nashville: Abingdon, 1996.

Suetonius. *The Twelve Caesars*. Translated by Robert Graves. Revised by Michael Grant. New York: Penguin Books, 2003.

Tacitus. *The Annals*. Rev. ed. Oxford translation. BCL. London: Henry G. Bohn, 1854.

Thompson, Robin. "Healing at the Pool of Bethesda: A Challenge to Asclepius?" *BBR* 27 (2017): 65–84.

Vagi, David L. *Coinage and History of the Roman Empire*. 2 vols. Chicago: Fitzroy Dearborn, 1999.

Wallace, Daniel B. *Greek Grammar beyond the Basics: An Exegetical Syntax of the New Testament*. Grand Rapids: Zondervan, 1996.

Warden, Duane. "Imperial Persecution and the Dating of 1 Peter and Revelation." *JETS* 34 (June 1991): 203–12.

Wilson, Mark. "The Early Christians in Ephesus and the Date of Revelation, Again." *Neotestamenica* 39 (2005): 163–93.

Witherington, Ben. *Revelation*. NCBC. New York: Cambridge University Press, 2003.

Worth, Roland H., Jr. *The Seven Cities of the Apocalypse and Greco-Asian Culture*. Mahwah, NJ: Paulist, 1999.

Wright, N. T. *Jesus and the Victory of God*. COQG. Minneapolis: Fortress, 1996.

———. *Surprised by Hope: Rethinking Heaven, the Resurrection, and the Mission of the Church*. New York: HarperOne, 2008.

Wright, N. T., and Michael F. Bird. *The New Testament in Its World: An Introduction to the History, Literature, and Theology of the First Christians*. Grand Rapids: Zondervan, 2019.

Wright, R. B. "Psalms of Solomon: A New Translation and Introduction." *OTP* 2:639–70.

SUBJECT INDEX

SCRIPTURE & EXTRABIBLICAL SOURCES INDEX

Old Testament

New Testament

Apocrypha

Pseudepigrapha

Greco-Roman Literature